A FalconGuide® to the
Mount Baker–Mount Shuksan Area

Help Us Keep This Guide Up to Date

Every effort has been made by the author and editors to make this guide as accurate and useful as possible. However, many things can change after a guide is published—trails are rerouted, regulations change, techniques evolve, facilities come under new management, etc.

We would love to hear from you concerning your experiences with this guide and how you feel it could be improved and kept up to date. While we may not be able to respond to all comments and suggestions, we'll take them to heart and we'll also make certain to share them with the author. Please send your comments and suggestions to the following address:

The Globe Pequot Press
Reader Response/Editorial Department
P.O. Box 480
Guilford, CT 06437

Or you may e-mail us at:

editorial@GlobePequot.com

Thanks for your input, and happy trails!

A **FALCON** GUIDE ®

Exploring Series

A FalconGuide® to the Mount Baker– Mount Shuksan Area

A Guide to Exploring the Great Outdoors

Mike McQuaide

FALCON GUIDE®

GUILFORD, CONNECTICUT
HELENA, MONTANA

AN IMPRINT OF THE GLOBE PEQUOT PRESS

A FALCON GUIDE®

All photographs by the author
Maps by Robert B. Lindquist © The Globe Pequot Press

ISSN 1553-958X
ISBN 0-7627-3062-5

Manufactured in the United States of America
First Edition/First Printing

The author and The Globe Pequot Press assume no liability for accidents happening to, or injuries sustained by, readers who engage in the activities described in this book.

*This book is dedicated to
my five brothers and sisters—Chris, Tom, Pat, Kath and Sharon—
who never fail to amaze, awe, and inspire me with all that they do.
(And make me laugh a good deal of the time they're doing it, too.)*

Contents

Acknowledgments xi

Introduction 1

   Natural and Cultural History 2

   The Great Outdoors 8

   Trail Etiquette 10

   Getting Here 11

   Where to Go and What to Do 12

Summer/Fall 15

   North Side 15

      Driving Tour 15

      Easy Hikes and Walks 23

      Day Hikes 38

      Accessible Wilderness 68

      Photography 71

      Camping 72

      Backpacking 75

      Mountain Climbing and Scrambling 78

      River Rafting 85

      Biking 85

   South Side 89

      Driving Tour 89

      Easy Hikes and Walks 93

      Day Hikes 102

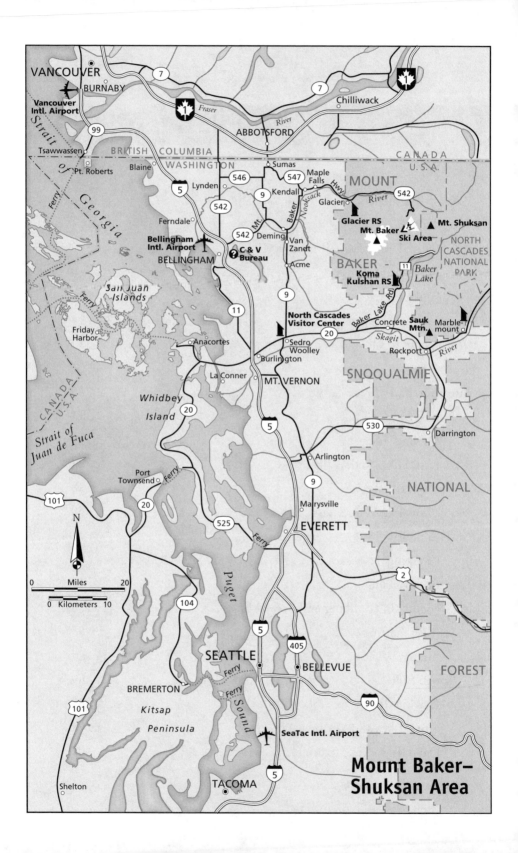

**Mount Baker–
Shuksan Area**

Nearby Hikes. 117

Accessible Wilderness 123

Worth Stopping. 124

Photography 124

Camping 125

Backpacking. 131

Mountain Climbing. 132

Canoeing and Kayaking 134

Fishing 137

Biking. 137

Winter/Spring. 139

North Side 139

Mount Baker Ski Area. 139

Heather Meadows 145

Backcountry Excursions 146

Winter Hiking 156

Eagle Viewing 157

South Side 159

Backcountry Excursions 159

Winter Hiking. 164

Canoeing and Kayaking 165

Eagle Viewing 166

Dining and Lodging 169

Annual Events 171

For More Information. 172

Index. 174

About the Author 179

Map Legend

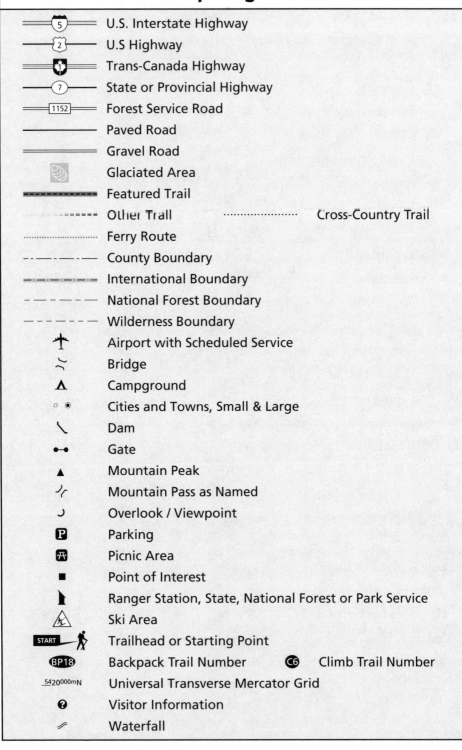

═══5═══	U.S. Interstate Highway
───2───	U.S Highway
═══🍁═══	Trans-Canada Highway
───7───	State or Provincial Highway
═══1152═══	Forest Service Road
───────	Paved Road
═══════	Gravel Road
	Glaciated Area
▬▬▬▬▬▬	Featured Trail
-------	Other Trail
···············	Ferry Route
—·—·—·	County Boundary
▬·▬·▬·▬	International Boundary
— — — —	National Forest Boundary
- - - - -	Wilderness Boundary
✈	Airport with Scheduled Service
≍	Bridge
⋀	Campground
° ◉	Cities and Towns, Small & Large
＼	Dam
•–•	Gate
▲	Mountain Peak
⅄	Mountain Pass as Named
⌐	Overlook / Viewpoint
🅿	Parking
⊞	Picnic Area
■	Point of Interest
▮	Ranger Station, State, National Forest or Park Service
⚠	Ski Area
START 🚶	Trailhead or Starting Point
BP18	Backpack Trail Number
5420000mN	Universal Transverse Mercator Grid
❷	Visitor Information
⁄⁄	Waterfall

·················· Cross-Country Trail

C6 Climb Trail Number

Acknowledgments

I want to thank the following individuals and organizations for offering their support, expertise, and/or friendship: Frank Schultz, Doug McKeever, Tim Schultz, Bud Hardwick, the Steeles, J. McQ and Baker, too, The Bottle Sprockets, Margaret Gerard, Nancy Lawrence, Montrail, Ultimate Direction, Smartwool, and the fine people at FalconGuide.

Table Mountain

Introduction

In the far northwest corner of Washington State, two geologic giants—10,781-foot Mount Baker and 9,131-foot Mount Shuksan—tower high above their North Cascade Mountain siblings. Thousands of feet higher than anything around them, with their majestic and regal twin visages, they appear watchful, as if keeping tabs on the countless creek and river valleys, ridgetop meadows, alpine lakes, and craggy peaks that surround them on all sides.

Visible on clear days to Seattleites 100 miles south and Vancouverites 80 miles west, Mounts Baker and Shuksan form the centerpiece of a roughly 400-square-mile area that's a year-round recreational wonderland. More than 200 miles of world-class walking, hiking, and backpacking trails crisscross the area through everything from ancient forests draped in mosses, subalpine meadows awash in wildflowers, and skyline ridges ending at the toes of icy glaciers. It's a true mecca for sightseers, photographers, backpackers, mountaineers, back-country skiers and snowboarders, and more.

It's also the site of the Mount Baker Ski Area, renowned for its steep, deep terrain and for being one of the birthplaces of snowboarding. Since 1999 it also has been the world record holder for annual snowfall. During the 1998–1999 ski and snowboard season, the area was blanketed by 95 feet of snow. In February alone, the sky dumped more than 300 inches of new snow.

Though just 10 miles apart as the raven flies, Mount Baker and Mount Shuksan couldn't be more geologically different. Ask a five-year-old to draw you a mountain and she'll likely draw something that looks a lot like Mount Baker—roughly, a symmetrical bell-shaped curve typical of Cascade strato-volcanoes. As for color, given that Baker's upper 5,000 feet are covered in glacier and permanent snowfield, a single white crayon should do.

Ask that same child to draw Mount Shuksan and your only hope is that she's a child prodigy. Not a volcano but rather the end result of millions of years of rock faults thrusting and shifting, Mount Shuksan is an elegant and dramatic mix of jagged edges, hanging glaciers, rumbling avalanches, and eerie blue ice. Aesthetically, it's one of Mother Nature's greatest hits and as such is often referred to as the most photographed mountain in the world, gracing countless calendars, postcards, and photo books.

From Artist Point in the Heather Meadows Area at the end of the Mount Baker Highway, visitors have spectacular, full-face views of both of these giants. Looking from one to the other, as you inevitably find yourself doing at Artist Point, you kind of feel like you're watching a tennis match; neck fatigue can be an issue.

The Mount Baker–Mount Shuksan area encompassed by this book includes the mountains themselves and the roughly 400-square-mile area surrounding them. This area stretches from the national forest boundary near the town of Glacier to the west; the United States–Canada border to the north; Baker Lake Dam to the south; and to the east, an imaginary line inside North Cascades National Park about 5 miles east of the Mount Shuksan massif. This area has no single park designation (i.e., there is no Mount Baker–Mount Shuksan National Park), but most of the area is managed by Mount Baker–Snoqualmie National Forest and North Cascades National Park. Within the national forest rubric, the land falls under designations such as Mount Baker Wilderness Area, Heather Meadows, and the Mount Baker National Recreation Area.

There are two main roads into the area. On the north side, access is from the Mount Baker Highway (Highway 542); on the south side, it's Baker Lake Road (off Highway 20) that provides the way in. And on both the north and south side, numerous Forest Service roads provide access to a variety of back-country activities.

Natural and Cultural History

Formed less than 30,000 years ago, Mount Baker is among the youngest of the fourteen Cascade volcanoes that range from Washington State to northern California. In fact it's only the most recent volcano that's occupied the site. The Black Buttes, jagged, rocky outcrops visible on Mount Baker's western flanks, are remnants of a much bigger volcano that formed here about half a million years ago.

While Mount Baker has never erupted a la Mount St. Helens, about 10,000 years ago, lava flowed down the south side of the mountain from a small cinder cone—a kind of parasitic minivolcano—near today's Schreibers Meadow, a popular hiking area. In the 1840s a major blast of steam erupted from Sherman Crater, the 1,200-foot-wide "bite" about 1,000 feet below the summit on Mount Baker's south side. Forest fires followed, as well as a major fish kill in nearby Baker River, and ash was spread throughout the landscape.

These days, steam can often be seen rising from the crater, particularly in winter. In 1975, five years before Mount St. Helens blew, increased heat, gas, and steam activity in the crater caused a major steam plume, melted glacial snow near the summit, and caused such concern that officials closed the nearby Baker Lake area to public access. The water level of the dam-impeded lake was lowered 10 feet; in the event of an eruption, the attendant avalanches, lahars (mud and debris flows), and flooded creeks and rivers would fill the lake to overflowing in no time.

Volcanologists and other scientists flocked to the area to monitor the mountain's geothermal activity. Mount Baker never blew, but five years later, in 1980, Mount St. Helens, a similar-size volcano less than 200 miles to the south, erupted cataclysmically, its upper 1,300 feet sheared off in the process. Still, Mount Baker remains an active volcano and is monitored closely.

Mount Shuksan, on the other hand, is not a volcano. Its Native American name means, according to one source, "roaring mountain"—a reference to the avalanches that crash down from its hanging glaciers and steep snow chutes. Other sources say Shuksan means "place of the storm wind" or "rocky and precipitous," both of which are apt descriptions. Unlike Mount Baker, Mount Shuksan is not new to the area, and its history is one of slow (read: *slooooow*) transformation. Geologists date the Shuksan greenschist, of which the mountain is mostly comprised, to 150 million years ago when it was basalt *located at the bottom of the ocean!* Nearby rocks have been dated to 225 million years ago.

Native Americans called Mount Baker "Koma Kulshan," which, depending on your source, means variously "the white watcher," "the shining one," or refers to a peak that has been damaged or exploded. Mount Baker was given its present moniker by George Vancouver, the famed British explorer. In 1792 he and his crew sailed east into what's now the Strait of Juan de Fuca on their voyage to survey the Pacific Northwest coast. While anchored near Dungeness Spit, about 100 miles southwest of the icy peak across Puget Sound, third lieutenant Joseph Baker spotted the mountain while taking his turn as the ship's watch. As a reward, Vancouver named the mountain for him.

Glaciers

At first glance, both Mount Shuksan and Mount Baker appear to be slathered with liberal amounts of white cake frosting. Alas, they're not. Rather they're mantled with frosty white glaciers, permanent (or at least long-lasting) accumulations of snow and ice that move ever so slowly down the mountain.

Very simply, glaciers form when more snow falls in winter than melts in summer. As this happens over a number of years and the snow level deepens, the bottom layers harden into a dense layer of ice. As the weight of the snow above increases, it pushes down on the layers below and the mass begins slowly creeping down the mountain.

Over time, as the ice becomes so dense that all air is forced out of the tiny pockets between the ice crystals, the ice absorbs all the colors of the spectrum except for blue, which it reflects. That's why glaciers often appear blue.

The North Cascades are the most heavily glaciated mountains in the Lower 48. And with 20 square miles of icy snow on its flanks, Mount Baker's thirteen glaciers boast more glacial area than all other Cascades volcanoes put together save for Mount Rainier. Because Mount Shuksan is not a gentle sloping volcano but rather a jagged, multilayered rock massif, its seven glaciers aren't quite as large as those on Baker, but they're perhaps more dramatic. Several of its glaciers appear to be in midtumble, with seracs—giant ice blocks—peeling off as they rumble down the mountain. The aptly named Hanging Glacier and the White Salmon Glacier, the ones most likely to attract your eye from Heather Meadows, are two examples.

Heather Meadows and Artist Point are prime glacier-viewing spots. To get a more up close and personal view of Mount Baker's glaciers, head to the Railroad Grade Trail (Hike 25) on the south side of the mountain or the Heliotrope Ridge Trail (Hike 9) accessed via Glacier Creek Road on the northwest side of the mountain. The popular Lake Ann Trail (Hike 17), accessed from the Heather Meadows area above Austin Pass, leads to gorgeous stare-up-in-wonder views seemingly directly below Mount Shuksan's Upper and Lower Curtis Glaciers.

But beware. Glaciers are potentially extremely dangerous. Do not climb on a glacier unless you have an ice ax, are roped up, and have prior glacier travel experience. Glaciers are riddled with crevasses, both ones that are visible and ones that are hidden below layers of snow. And they're deep, some 100 feet or more. Falls into crevasses are often fatal.

The First to the Top

In the latter half of the nineteenth century, Whatcom County and the waterfront town of Bellingham were being settled, driven largely by the area's vast timber resources and by folks with dreams of striking it rich by finding gold in the nearby Cascade Mountains. Inevitably, Mounts Baker and Shuksan caught the eye of adventurous mountaineering types eager to be the first to the top. (There are no records of early Native Americans summiting either mountain.)

Perhaps because of its greater visibility to lowland dwellers hundreds of miles around and because its mostly symmetrical, "gentler" volcanic shape appeared less technical, Mount Baker inspired early and numerous attempts. Edmund Coleman, an Englishman who settled in Victoria, British Columbia, from which he had admired the mountain, reached the summit of Mount Baker in 1868 after two unsuccessful attempts two years earlier.

On Coleman's first attempt from the south via the Skagit and Baker Rivers, he was forced to turn back by local Native Americans. On his second attempt that year, this time from the northwest, he got maddeningly close to the summit, but bad weather and a dangerous overhanging ice cornice forced him to retreat just a few hundred feet shy of his goal. The third time proved a charm, and on August 17, 1868, Coleman, along with climbing partners John Tennant,

Northwest Forest Pass

To park at almost all of the trailheads and picnic sites in this book, you'll need a Northwest Forest Pass. Cost is $5.00 for a daily pass or $30.00 for an annual pass. Passes are available at the Glacier Public Service Center, at the Forest Service office in Sedro-Woolley, and at many local businesses located near the national forest. They're also available online through www.naturenw .org, www.wta.org, and the Mount Baker–Snoqualmie National Forest Service Web site at www.fs.fed.us/r6/mbs. Revenue from pass sales goes to trail and picnic site maintenance.

David Ogilvy, and Thomas Stratton, made it to the highest point in the northwest corner of the Pacific Northwest.

These days Mount Baker is one of the most popular climbing destinations in the Cascades, with hundreds making for the summit each year, most during the summer. One of the two popular routes is the Coleman-Deming Glacier Route, basically the same route that the original Edmund Coleman party used.

In 1906, almost forty years after the successful Coleman climb on Mount Baker, noted Northwest photographer Asahel Curtis and companion W. Montelius Price were the first to make it to the top of Mount Shuksan's summit pyramid. However, some say that mountain man "Mighty" Joe Morovits, a prospector, trailblazer, and mountain guide who homesteaded in the meadows between Mount Baker and Mount Shuksan, was the first person to the summit of the latter, possibly as early as 1897.

Becoming a Tourist Destination

Mountaineers were not the only ones drawn to the Mount Baker–Shuksan area. In the latter half of the nineteenth century, miners in search of gold, loggers in search of trees (which were everywhere), homesteaders, and others began showing up not just in what would become Bellingham but also in settlements along the Nooksack River closer to the mountains. Road building improved also, and in the 1870s and '80s there was a push to build a road that would one day span the North Cascades into eastern Washington. (That wouldn't happen for almost eighty years, and it would be about 30 miles south of where civic leaders were hoping it would go.)

By 1896 a road reached all the way from Bellingham on Puget Sound to the now defunct mining town site of Shuksan, about 50 miles away. (It's near the present-day Silver Fir Campground, about milepost 46 on the Mount Baker Highway.) But that's as far as it went for about twenty-five years, until the mid-1920s when some Bellingham developers formed the Mount Baker Development

Company. They made an agreement with the Forest Service (of the federal government) to build a lodge in return for a road that would lead 9 winding, 2,000-foot-climbing miles to a selected site at about 4,500 feet.

In 1927 the highway to the posh Mount Baker Lodge, located near the present-day ski area, opened to great fanfare. Each of the lodge's one hundred rooms had hot and cold running water and a telephone, which is more than can be said of the spot today. (Even today there is no landline phone service at the Mount Baker Ski Area, the area's only present-day concession.) Many of the trails in the area, such as those around Table Mountain and Bagley Lakes, were completed at this time for guests to enjoy. The highway's final 3 miles to Artist Point were completed in 1929.

Oddly, given the area's present-day reputation as a winter wonderland and one of snowboarding's places of origin, the lodge was a summer resort only. (The Mount Baker Ski Area wouldn't take shape for another twenty-five years.) It opened in June and closed just after Labor Day.

The lavish lodge offered miniature golf, sightseeing, boating, swimming, hiking, fishing, and guided mountain climbing. Unfortunately, in 1931 it burned to the ground in an electrical fire. But with its good road built high into a wonderful subalpine area and skiing, hiking, and sightseeing somewhat established, Heather Meadows and Artist Point continued to grow in reputation as a regional tourist destination.

Hollywood Finds the Mountains

It wasn't long before this new, relatively easy high-mountain access began to draw Hollywood film productions. First there was *Wolf Fangs* in 1927, a feature about a dog named Thunder who left his human family for the lure of the wilderness. For the shoot, more than 500 sheep and 30 dogs were transported to the meadows.

Next was *The Call of the Wild* in 1934, starring Clark Gable and Loretta Young. Based on the classic Jack London adventure novel set in Alaska (and once again focusing on a dog), the film was at the time one of Hollywood's biggest-budget movies. Filming took place at the Heather Meadows Area and the Nooksack River about 8 miles back down the road in the valley. Because it was a winter shoot, the road to Heather Meadows was plowed throughout the winter for the first time.

In 1937 Heather Meadows once again stood in for Alaska when the gold-rush pic *The Barrier* was filmed there. In contrast to *Call of the Wild*, this was a summertime shoot, and the crew had to work around the summertime sightseers and picnickers, many of whom were curious and tended to get in the way.

The area became a movie set once again in the late 1970s when scenes from *The Deer Hunter* were shot here. Scenes were also shot high on Glacier Creek

Road. Oddly enough, the location was supposed to be depicting western Pennsylvania.

Mount Baker Marathon and Ski to Sea

In the early 1900s, before the road to Heather Meadows and the Mount Baker Lodge was built, civic leaders in Bellingham made a push for the Mount Baker area to be designated as a national park. The Mount Baker Club, a group of Whatcom County outdoor recreation–minded business leaders, formed with the hopes that with the lure of a national park in its backyard, Bellingham and Whatcom County would become a real tourist destination. They were encouraged by what had happened to local communities near Mount Rainier after it became a national park in 1899. (The club still exists today though with a different focus; it's called the Mount Baker Hiking Club.)

To publicize the idea, the Mount Baker Club came up with the idea for the Mount Baker Marathon, a race from Bellingham to the top of Mount Baker and back in which competitors were allowed to use any mode of conveyance that they wished. To get from Bellingham to the trails leading to the mountain, racers could ride the 44-mile Bellingham Bay and British Columbia Railroad to the town of Glacier (from there it was 14 miles one way up wooded trail and glacier, a 28-mile run-hike-climb round-trip to the summit), or they could drive 26 miles on road to a local ranch just west of the mountain and run-hike-climb 16 miles (32 miles round-trip) through forest and glacier to the top.

Given that the upper 5,000 feet or so of Mount Baker is heavily glaciated—much of it riddled with crevasses—not to mention prone to avalanche, it's not surprising that this race was held only three times before being discontinued for safety reasons. In the 1913 race a racer fell 40 feet into a crevasse and almost froze to death as he waited some six hours to be rescued. The Mount Baker Marathon was never held again.

In 1973, however, a spirit of the race was revived with the initiation of the now annual Ski to Sea relay race. Held Memorial Day weekend, Ski to Sea is the centerpiece of Bellingham and Whatcom County's biggest community event. Instead of individuals racing to and from Mount Baker's summit, more than 300 relay teams of eight people cross-country ski, downhill ski, run, road bike, canoe, mountain bike, and kayak an 80-mile course from the Mount Baker Ski Area to Marine Park on Bellingham Bay. Along with almost 2,500 race participants, more than 100,000 people converge on the area for a weeklong celebration featuring fairs, concerts, art shows, and more.

The early Mount Baker Marathons brought publicity to the area, but they didn't bring the mountain or the area national park status. Concerns over the mining and logging restrictions that would be imposed if it were to become a national park stalled the movement, as did the approach of World War I. The area remained under the jurisdiction of the national forest.

In 1968, however, 684,000-acre North Cascades National Park was signed into existence. It included Mount Shuksan but oddly not Mount Baker. Lobbying by area conservationists paid off in 1984, when 117,500 acres of national forest in the Mount Baker area—including most of Mount Baker itself—much of it bordering the national park to the west, was proclaimed the Mount Baker Wilderness Area. The goal of wilderness is to manage human use so that it doesn't alter natural processes. No logging or mining can take place, and motorized vehicles are not allowed into the backcountry.

In conjunction with the wilderness act, also in 1984, the Mount Baker National Recreation Area was created so that winter snowmobile use could legally continue on the south side of Mount Baker in the Schreibers Meadow area.

The Great Outdoors

Wildlife

Depending on the season, a visit to the Mount Baker–Mount Shuksan area will likely yield views of everything from a pileated woodpecker working up one heck of a headache on a decades-old snag to cheeky, chubby hoary marmots scampering into a hole after letting out ear-piercing whistles; great horned owls patrolling ancient forests to stately mountain goats tiptoeing across rocky talus slopes; tiny, food-stealing, mouse-size pikas; and the white-tailed ptarmigan who turn white in winter to match the snow, brown in summer to blend in with the rocks.

Stellar's jays, ravens, black-tailed deer, American dippers, foxes, chinook and coho salmon, ospreys, bald eagles, and Roosevelt elk are just some of the nearly 300 bird, mammal, fish, reptile, and amphibian species that call the alpine heights and dark river valleys of this area home. And while none have been spotted in this area for some time, grizzly bears and gray wolves once roamed the area, and some people suspect that they still do.

And of course, depending on how far into the backcountry you venture, there's always the chance for an encounter with the two species most likely to cause increased heart rate and adrenal secretions: black bears and cougars. Cougar sightings are extremely rare, and in most instances a bear will quickly run away when it becomes aware of your presence. Nevertheless, should you encounter a bear or cougar, heed the following tips from the U.S. Department of Fish and Wildlife.

Bear: Respect a bear's personal space, and give it plenty of room to get away. Avoid direct eye contact with the bear, and speak softly to it while at the same time backing away from it. Don't turn your back on it, and try not to show fear. If it won't leave you alone and you absolutely can't get away from it, try to scare it by yelling or clapping your hands. If the bear attacks, fight back using anything at your disposal. Should the attack continue, curl up in a ball or lie down on your stomach and play dead. Also, never get between a cub and its mother.

Cougar: Should you encounter a cougar, keep direct eye contact with it while slowly backing away. Raise your arms above your head, open your jacket if you're wearing one, and wave a stick above your head—anything to make yourself appear larger. If the cougar approaches, yell and throw rocks, sticks, or anything you can get your hands on. If it attacks, fight back aggressively.

Flora

What are those trees? Dreams of getting rich by striking gold might have been what lured many of the first settlers to this corner of Washington about 150 years ago, but it was the prodigious amounts of available lumber—massive Douglas firs, western red cedars, and western hemlocks—in the lowlands that kept them here.

In the Baker–Shuksan area covered in this book, the lower-elevation river valleys are rich in the aforementioned firs, cedars, and hemlocks, as well as alders and vine maples. A couple places—Shadow of the Sentinels off Baker Lake Road on the south side and North Fork Nooksack Research Natural Area—offer easy rain forest walks through ancient cathedrals of massive moss-hung firs and cedars more than 700 years old. Sword ferns, bunchberry, trillium, wild ginger, maidenhair ferns, salmonberry, devil's club, and various mosses and lichens with names such as old-man's beard are some of the plants and flowers that share these lower-elevation forests.

In higher elevations—above 3,000 feet—trees such as mountain hemlock, subalpine fir, and Pacific silver fir predominate. In summer and fall, red, yellow, and white heathers are also common in this subalpine region—especially at places such as aptly named Heather Meadows—and so are big huckleberry and Cascade blueberries. Along with providing a dazzling red to the subalpine's spectacular fall colors, the latter two offer a tasty mountain treat. In summer, subalpine meadows come alive with bursts of color from wildflowers such as Indian paintbrush, mountain daisy, Columbia tiger lily, western anemone, avalanche lily, and subalpine lupine.

Insects

Yes, heavy rainfall means abundant snow in the mountains, raging rivers in the valleys, and plunging waterfalls everywhere. In summer, it means something else, too—bugs, particularly relentless swarms of black flies on the mountain trails.

Here's the chronology: The snow lingers long above 4,000 feet (especially on north-facing slopes), and when enough of it finally melts for the trails to become passable (say, July or August) it's prime time for black flies, which can be extremely pesky, annoying, and maddening.

To lessen their impact, carry bug repellent of some sort (DEET works but can be fairly industrial strength), wear clothing that covers your arms and legs, and hike earlier in the day before bugs have a chance to get up and about. (If you're so inclined, run parts of the trails—I'm an avid trail runner and almost never have problems with flies.) They're less present when it's breezy out and at mountain passes, too. Luckily, they don't stay around forever and are usually not a problem come early fall.

Weather

Wet down low; snowy up high. The Northwest is renowned for its prodigious rainfall, and at higher elevations—and this far north—that precip is likely to take the form of snow. In fact, above 5,000 feet (Artist Point is at 5,100) snow is possible every day of the year, though it occurs with more regularity from November through April. The Mount Baker Ski Area, which is located in the Heather Meadows Area, receives about 600 inches of snow per year and during the 1998–1999 season received 1,140 inches—95 feet!—a world record. Because of such snowfall, the last 3 miles of the Mount Baker Highway—from the ski area to Artist Point—are snowbound most of the year. Most years it's plowed and open to cars from sometime in July until sometime in October.

Spring and fall are pleasant—just carry a sweater and/or some kind of rain-resistant jacket or shell—and summer is downright glorious. Here's a secret: From mid-July through late September, it almost never rains, and daytime temperatures are usually in the 70s and 80s.

In winter, despite the wet stuff down low and white stuff up high, it rarely gets brutally cold. Temperatures at high elevations, even in midwinter, rarely go lower than the teens, with upper 20s, low 30s more common. Winter temps at lower elevations covered in this book are usually in the high 30s to high 40s.

Trail Etiquette

Zero impact. Always leave an area just like you found it—if not better than you found it. Avoid camping in fragile, alpine meadows and along the banks of streams and lakes. Use a camp stove versus building a wood fire. Pack up all of your trash and extra food. Bury human waste at least 100 feet from water sources under 6 to 8 inches of topsoil. Don't bathe with soap in a lake or stream—use prepackaged moistened towels to wipe off sweat and dirt, or bathe in the water without soap.

Stay on the trail. It's true, a path anywhere leads nowhere new, but purists will just have to get over it. Paths serve an important purpose; they limit impact on natural areas. Straying from a designated trail may seem innocent but it can cause damage to sensitive areas—damage that may take years to recover, if it can recover at all. Even simple shortcuts can be destructive. So, please, stay on the trail.

Leave no weeds. Noxious weeds tend to overtake other plants, which in turn affects animals and birds that depend on them for food. To minimize the spread of noxious weeds, hikers should regularly clean their boots, tents, packs, and hiking poles of mud and seeds. Also brush your dog to remove any weed seeds before heading off into a new area.

Keep your dog under control. You can buy a retractable-cord leash that allows your dog to go exploring along the trail, while allowing you the ability to reel him in should another hiker approach or should he decide to chase a rabbit. Always obey leash laws and be sure to bury your dog's waste or pack it in resealable plastic bags. Some trails/areas do not allow dogs.

Respect other trail users. Often you're not the only one on the trail. With the rise in popularity of multiuse trails, you'll have to learn a new kind of respect, beyond the nod and "hello" approach you may be used to. First investigate whether you're on a multiuse trail, and assume the appropriate precautions. When you approach horses or pack animals on the trail, always step quietly off the trail, preferably on the downhill side, and let them pass. If you're wearing a large backpack, it's often a good idea to sit down. To some animals, a hiker wearing a large backpack might appear threatening.

Getting Here

This book focuses on two access roads: the Mount Baker Highway (Highway 542) at the north end and Baker Lake Road at the south.

To Reach the Mount Baker Highway

From the east: Head west on Highway 20 (North Cascades Highway) to Interstate 5 in Burlington. Go north on I–5 for 25 miles to Bellingham exit 255 and the Mount Baker Highway. For the Mount Baker-Mount Shuksan area covered in this book, follow the highway east for about 33 miles to the town of Glacier.

From the south: Head north on I–5 to Bellingham exit 255. For the rest of the way, follow directions from the east.

From the north: Head south on I–5 to Bellingham exit 255. For the rest of the way, follow directions from the east.

From the west: Head east on the Mount Baker Highway from the junction with I–5 exit 255.

To Reach Baker Lake Road

From the east: Go west on Highway 20 to milepost 82.3 and turn right onto Baker Lake Road. Head north for about 12 miles to the first of the sites listed in this book.

From the south: Head north on I–5 to Burlington and exit 230. Go east on Highway 20 for about 25 miles to milepost 82.3 and Baker Lake Road. Turn left and head north.

From the north: Head south on I–5 to Burlington and exit 230. For the rest of the way, follow directions from the south.

From the west: Go east on Highway 20 from Burlington for about 25 miles to milepost 82.3 and Baker Lake Road. Turn left and head north.

Where to Go and What to Do

North Side (Mount Baker Scenic Byway and Heather Meadows Area)

For the purposes of this book, all mentions of the Mount Baker Highway refer to the last 24 miles of the road, from mileposts 33 to 57 (roughly from Glacier to Artist Point). This stretch is also known as the Mount Baker Scenic Byway.

For much of the way from Glacier to Artist Point, the Mount Baker Highway follows the North Fork of the Nooksack River. The road gains about 4,100 feet of elevation over this stretch—most of that in the last 10 miles when it breaks away from the river—and along the way offers access to a wide range of year-round activities. Higher elevations—closer to Artist Point, Heather Meadows, and the Mount Baker Ski Area—are jumping-off points for hiking, backpacking, nonstrenuous sightseeing, downhill skiing, snowboarding, and snowshoeing. Lower elevations—closer to Glacier—present opportunities for river rafting, cross-country skiing, wildlife viewing, mountain biking, fishing, sightseeing, lowland hiking, and more.

Always a stunning drive any time of year, the paved two-lane road winds its way along the Nooksack River gorge, passing through stretches of dense forest, and from time to time offering ever-closer views of Mount Baker's icy flanks. Along the byway, you'll find trailheads, campgrounds, and Forest Service roads to trails, as well as good places to just pull off and gaze into the rushing Nooksack as it snakes through its gorge.

You won't find gas stations, however. The last is in Maple Falls, at about milepost 26. And after the town of Glacier, about 7 miles past Maple Falls, the only place to get something to eat is at the Mount Baker Ski Area (at mileposts 52 and 55), which is usually open from late November through the end of April. Glacier itself, however, despite its tiny population, has some surprisingly good restaurants, a general store with lots of character and history, and ski and snowboard shops.

The last 10 miles of the Mount Baker Highway climb 3,000 feet, much of it via a series of hairpin turns with steep cliffs, sharp drop-offs, and no guardrails. Concentration is key, especially since it's along this stretch that Mount Shuksan's spectacular form—yet another distraction—first comes into view. The road ends at Artist Point on a 5,100-foot ridge between 10,781-foot Mount Baker and 9,131-foot Mount Shuksan. It's one of the highest points in Washington State accessible by road. You're in alpine splendor here with 360-degree mountain and valley views, and it's easily one of the most scenic drive-up spots in the entire country, let alone the Northwest.

Heavy snowpack closes the last 3 miles of the byway for nine or ten months a year. (How heavy is the snowpack? Most years about 600 inches of snow fall here—that's 50 feet.) But the road is plowed and stays open year-round to at least the Mount Baker Ski Area upper lodge parking area, at milepost 55.

The last 4 miles of the Mount Baker Highway, from just below the ski area to Artist Point, pass through the Heather Meadows Area, which offers some of the best and most easily accessible sightseeing, hiking, and snow fun in the North Cascades. From here, hiking trails and barrier-free walks lead onto the flanks of both Mount Baker and Mount Shuksan. The Heather Meadows Visitor Center, staffed by Forest Service employees and volunteers, offers interpretive displays, guided walks, and a gift shop. The center is open from mid-July through late fall.

South Side (Baker Lake Road and Baker Lake Basin)

Approaching the Mount Baker–Mount Shuksan area from the south, 26-mile-long Baker Lake Road is accessed via Highway 20 (North Cascades Highway) at about milepost 82.3, roughly 15 miles east of Sedro-Woolley. Unlike the Mount Baker Highway, Baker Lake Road does not climb particularly high, topping out at about 1,100 feet and for most of the way remains a few hundred feet lower than that, thus it can be snow-free almost the entire year.

Consequently, for higher-elevation fun—such as alpine hiking, mountain climbing, backpacking, backcountry skiing, and snowboarding—you have to work a little harder than you do from the Mount Baker Highway, either by driving Forest Service roads that get you into the high country, or hiking on trails that do the same.

By its very name, Baker Lake Road hints at something it's got that the south side has that the north side doesn't: a lake. In fact, there are two—Lake Shannon is the other, but because that lake is not on public land, this book won't concern itself too much with Lake Shannon.

In 1959 Puget Power, a regional energy company, built a hydroelectric dam at the south end of what was a much smaller Baker Lake than the 5,000-plus-acre one that exists today. Trees in the basin were logged prior to flooding so that even today when the lake's water level is low, hundreds of stumps can be seen rising from the lake bottom. Today the lake offers great canoeing and fishing, and the 10-mile lakeshore is dotted with campgrounds, especially on its west side.

Forest Service roads lead from the lakeside to numerous hiking and equestrian trails on the southern flanks of both Mount Baker and Mount Shuksan as well as nearby ridges and crags. For those heading to the summits of Baker or Shuksan, two of the more popular and least technical climbing routes start here on the south sides on the mountains. The Mount Baker National Recreation Area, which allows the use of snowmobiling, is also accessed here.

How to Use the Maps

The maps in this book that depict a detailed close-up of an area use elevation tints, called hypsometry, to portray relief. Each gray tone represents a range of equal elevation, as shown in the scale key with the map. These maps will give you a good idea of elevation gain and loss. The darker tones are lower elevations and the lighter grays are higher elevations. The lighter the tone, the higher the elevation. Narrow bands of different gray tones spaced closely together indicate steep terrain, whereas wider bands indicate areas of more gradual slope.

Maps that show larger geographic areas use shaded, or shadow, relief. Shadow relief does not represent elevation; it demonstrates slope or relative steepness. This gives an almost 3-D perspective of the physiography of a region and will help you see where ranges and valleys are.

Summer/Fall

Summers can be short in this northwest corner of the Northwest, but they sure are sweet. Yes, this area is renowned for its rain and record snows, but here's a secret (one that locals would rather didn't get out): From about mid-July through the end of August, it almost never rains. Let me amend that—it never rains. Blue skies are pretty much guaranteed, and temperatures, while they occasionally top 80, are more likely to be 70s and high 60s. In short, it's glorious. (Oddly, June can be one of the rainiest months of the year. Or maybe it just seems that way.)

Higher up the mountain, it's likely to be a few degrees cooler, but not always. At least once or twice a summer, a high-pressure front plants itself over the entire Northwest, bathing all elevations in a week of 80-degree temperatures, no wind, and views seemingly all the way to California.

Note: Because the snow lasts year-round at higher elevations, eye and skin protection is extremely important. Snow reflects the bright sun and multiplies its UV radiation, and can result in some nasty sunburns and/or squinting. Come prepared.

The beautiful summer weather often extends into September. Though with the days getting shorter, and quickly, evenings and mornings can be downright cold, especially at higher elevations. October weather is unsettled and November brings the rains and drizzles and showers and, higher up, the snow.

North Side

Driving Tour

The Mount Baker Highway is the north-side access to the Mount Baker–Mount Shuksan area. What follows are access points, listed by milepost number, of viewpoints, trailheads, picnic areas, and other points of interest. These are from the town of Glacier at milepost 33 (33 miles from Bellingham) to the road's end at Artist Point at milepost 57. *See map on pages 16–17.*

MP (Milepost) 33.3, Glacier: This town (population: not many) is the home of the world-famous Mount Baker Snowboard Shop and for a couple decades now the stomping grounds of some of snowboarding's pioneers and studs and stud-ettes. (It's also home of Milano's Restaurant and Deli, one of the author's two favorite restaurants in the world.)

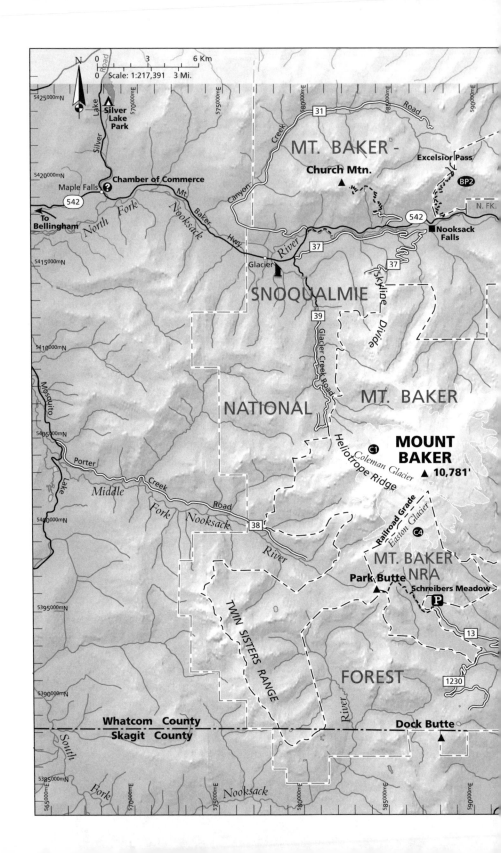

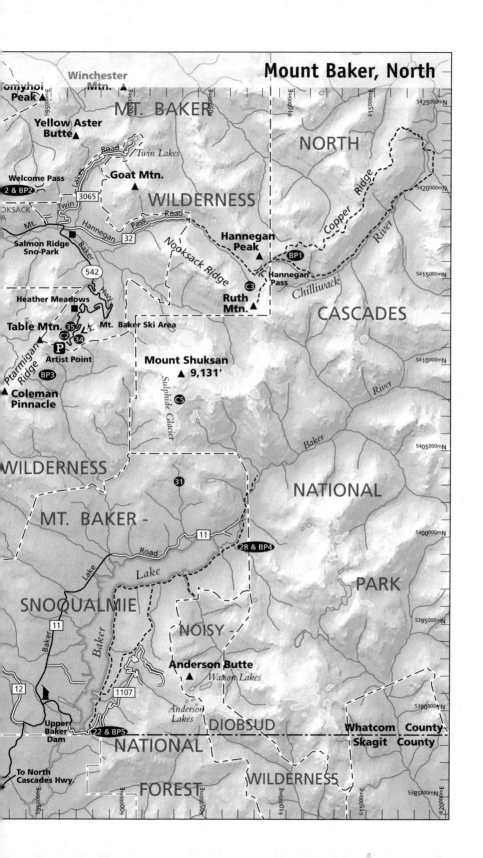

Mount Baker, North

It has the last services on the Mount Baker Highway, too. You'll find food (Graham Store makes a great end-of-day stop for ice cream or place to stock up for hiking), lodging, and ski and snowboard shops—but no gas. For that you'll need to head back west toward Bellingham about 7 miles to Maple Falls.

MP 33.6, Glacier Public Service Center: Stop here to find out the latest trail conditions, purchase a Northwest Forest Pass (required for parking at Forest Service trailheads and the Heather Meadows Area), or pick up maps, postcards, and books about the area. Check out the fun hands-on relief display of the area's mountains, valleys, rivers, and lakes on which you can pretend your fingers are people hiking the trails or skiing the slopes.

Outside, find interpretive signs and maps, a Northwest Forest Pass vending machine, picnic tables, restrooms, and a slice cut from a giant fir tree that was already into its third century when Shakespeare was writing about melancholy Danes and star-crossed lovers. The stone and cedar-shingled building that houses the center was built in 1939 by the Civilian Conservation Corps (CCC) and is on the National Register of Historic Places. It's one of several CCC buildings and campsites in the area.

The center is open daily from Memorial Day through mid-November and on some weekends during the rest of the year. Call (360) 599–2714 for more information.

MP 34.3, Glacier Creek Road (Forest Service Road 39): This mostly paved road climbs 3,100 feet in 9 miles and, along with offering access to the popular Heliotrope Ridge Trail (see Hike 9), leads to a picnic area and viewpoint with awe-inspiring look-sees of Mount Baker, just 4 air miles away. That's actually 2 miles closer to the mountain than Artist Point. (Because the trees at the picnic area are becoming overgrown, the best views are from the side of the road about a quarter mile *before* the picnic tables.)

If you've seen *The Deer Hunter,* you might recognize this view. The scenes of hunting a deer (which is really a Roosevelt elk) that are supposed to take place in western Pennsylvania were shot here and near Artist Point. Grab a take-out bite in Glacier and cruise on up the hill—no pain, but lots of gain. (*Note:* Unlike the Mount Baker Highway, this road is not plowed year-round. Check with the ranger before driving up.)

MP 34.3: To reach Forest Service Road 37 (also known as Deadhorse Road), turn right onto Glacier Creek Road and then make a quick left onto a gravel road. This is FR 37. The Boyd Creek Interpretive and Skyline Divide Trails are accessed from FR 37 (see Hikes 1 and 10).

MP 35.3, Horseshoe Bend Trail: For great views of the rushing Nooksack River and of rafters and river kayakers getting bounced, bumped, and bruised while negotiating same, turn right into the roadside pullout area just after crossing the Nooksack River bridge. Descend a set of steps to the river's edge for close-up views of rushing glacial water hurrying and scurrying to get to Puget Sound. In the mood for more forest and water contemplation? Follow the 1.2-mile (each way) Horseshoe Bend Trail as it snakes along the river (see Hike 2). Because of its relatively low elevation, about 900 feet, this trail is passable almost year-round.

MP 35.3, Douglas Fir Campground: Located across the road from the Horseshoe Bend Trailhead, this campground has a day-use picnic area as well.

MP 35.4, Canyon Creek Road (Forest Service Road 31): This partially paved road leads about 15 miles and climbs about 3,000 feet as it eventually traverses the west and north sides of Church Mountain, about 2 miles south of the United States–Canada border. You'll find trailheads to Damfino Lakes and Excelsior Mountain, High Divide, Boundary Way, and also the rugged Canyon Ridge Trail, one of the only trails in the Mount Baker–Snoqualmie National Forest that allows mountain biking (though, in truth, the trail is so primitive and overgrown that it's probably not worth the effort). The higher elevations of Canyon Creek Road are snow-covered most of the year, and the road is prone to washouts. Again, check with the ranger for the latest conditions.

MP 37 to the end of the road: Along this stretch there are numerous pullouts for North Fork Nooksack River views and places for slower drivers to pull over and allow faster ones to pass.

MP 38.7, Church Mountain Road (Forest Service Road 3040): This gravel road leads 2.6 miles to popular Church Mountain Trail (see Hike 11), one of the first alpine trails to be clear of snow in the summer.

MP 39.8, Excelsior Group Campground: There are two large-group campsites here, each accomodating up to fifty campers (see Camping section later in this chapter).

MP 40.5, Nooksack Falls: Turn right onto Wells Creek Road (Forest Service Road 33) and continue 0.6 mile to a parking lot just before a bridge. Follow your ears to the sound of rushing water, and in just moments you'll be struck by the awe-inspiring views of two mighty threads of the Nooksack River plunging 170 feet off a rock cliff onto a jumble of boulders below. The view is made even more spectacular by Lower Wells Creek Falls, which cascade just to the south.

Unfortunately, because the views are partially blocked, some waterfall lovers have made bad choices in attempts to get a better look. In June of both 1998 and 1999, individuals ignored the multiple warning signs posted in the area and climbed past the safety fence, only to slip on moss-covered rocks and plunge to their deaths. So, stay behind the fence. Let me repeat, stay behind the fence. One more thing: Stay behind the fence.

MP 41.2, Excelsior Pass Trailhead: This is the only trail with Mount Baker Highway roadside access that begins in the Nooksack River valley and climbs to an alpine ridge. Not surprisingly, it's steep and strenuous (see Hike 12).

Wells Creek crashing near Nooksack Falls

MP 43.8, North Fork Nooksack Research Natural Area: Here you'll find an easy forest walk with roadside access through ancient trees, some more than 700 years old (see Hike 3).

MP 45.9, Forest Service Road 3060: This easy-to-miss primitive road leads 0.75 mile to the Welcome Pass Trailhead, a steep, strenuous trail that climbs to Welcome Pass and High Divide Ridge (see Hike 12).

MP 46.3, Twin Lakes Road (Forest Service Road 3065): This gravel road leads 7 miles to the eponymous Twin Lakes. However, the last 2.5 miles are extremely rough. Unless you have the most bomber, high-clearance SUV known to mankind, it's best to park at the Yellow Aster Butte Trailhead, about 4.5 miles along Twin Lakes Road, and hike the rest of the way to Twin Lakes. Along with the Yellow Aster Butte Trailhead, Twin Lakes Road leads to the Winchester Mountain Lookout, High Pass, Tomyhoi Lake, and Silesia Creek Trailheads.

MP 46.5, Hannegan Pass Road (Forest Service Road 32): Just beyond Twin Lakes Road, this gravel road offers access to Goat Mountain, Hannegan Pass, and Nooksack Cirque Trails. From Hannegan Pass, you can continue on the Copper Ridge Trail into North Cascades National Park. The Shuksan Picnic Area is accessed via Hannegan Pass Road, just beyond the intersection with the Mount Baker Highway. (See Hike 15 for more information on Hannegan Pass.)

MP 46.9, Salmon Ridge Sno-Park: On the left, Salmon Ridge is a popular winter destination for cross-country skiing and snowshoeing.

MP 46.9, Silver Fir Campground: This campground is just beyond Hannegan Pass Road on the right (see the Camping section later in this chapter).

MP 46.9, Anderson Creek Road: Just past the Silver Fir Campground, this road is popular with cross-country skiers and snowshoers.

MP 47: The Mount Baker Highway begins climbing in earnest, gaining 3,000 feet over the next 10.5 winding, snaking miles. There are steep drops and no guardrails—the scenery is spectacular, but keep your eyes on the road!

MP 48: Views of spectacular Mount Shuksan begin to emerge.

MP 51.5, Forest Service Road 3075: Located at a sharp bend in the road just past milepost 51, this gravel road (also known as White Salmon Road) contours along the side of the mountain for a couple miles and offers huge, full-face views of Mount Shuksan.

MP 52.1, The award-winning Mount Baker Ski Area White Salmon Day Lodge is also known as the lower lodge; closed during the summer and fall.

MP 52.9: Enter Heather Meadows. A Northwest Forest Pass is required to park along the remainder of the highway.

MP 54.1, Picture and Highwood Lakes: Here you'll see stunning views of Mount Shuksan and its reflection; this is the spot where most of the postcard, calendar, and magazine shots of the mountain are taken. There are many pull-out spots, a paved pathway, and picnic tables. A Northwest Forest Pass is required to park here.

Columnar basalt along the Mount Baker Highway

MP 54.6, Mount Baker Ski Area Heather Meadows Day Lodge: This lodge is closed during the summer and fall. From late October until sometime in July, the Mount Baker Highway closes just beyond the upper parking lot here because of heavy snowpack.

The following highway mileposts are applicable during the summer months when the last 3 miles are open.

MP 55.2, Heather Meadows Visitor Center and Austin Pass Picnic Area: Built in 1940 by the CCC, the stone and timber visitor center is perched on a rock ledge overlooking Bagley Lakes and boasts stunning views of Table Mountain and Mount Herman. Staffed by Forest Service employees and volunteers, the center offers interpretive displays, guided walks, and a gift shop. It's open from mid-July through late fall.

Just outside, the Austin Pass Picnic Area offers an out-of-this-world setting rich with mountains, lakes, and creeks that is perfect for noshing before heading out on one of the nearby trails or just relaxing and soaking in the scenery. Find interpretive signs explaining the local geology, flora, and fauna, and marking the trailheads for Wild Goose, Bagley Lakes, Fire and Ice (partially paved and entirely barrier-free), and Chain Lakes Trails.

MP 56, Lake Ann Trailhead: This trail leads to a magical alpine lake and the best front-row views of Mount Shuksan (see Hike 17).

MP 57, Artist Point: This is the end of the road. Perhaps fittingly, at Artist Point it's the first time you're treated to breathtaking views of both Mount Baker and Mount Shuksan from the same place. At 5,100 feet, Artist Point is one of the highest points accessible by road in the state. Truth be told, Artist Point itself is mostly just a giant parking lot with great views that's a jumping-off point for a number of trails. But oh, those views! And oh, those trails!

To the south, Mount Baker is just 6 air miles away; to the east, Mount Shuksan is less than half that. Hiking options here are numerous—Artist Ridge for closer views of Mount Shuksan, Ptarmigan Ridge to get close to Baker, Chain Lakes for alpine ponds hidden by the great prow of Table Mountain, Table Mountain for that top-of-the-world feeling.

Then again, if you're not in the mood for hiking, fret not. Play in the snow—there's almost always some snow here, and there's nothing quite like photos of August snowball fights or toboggan plunges. (For cheap fun, a plastic garbage bag makes for great snow sliding.) There's also a short, barrier-free paved path for those needing assistance.

Easy Hikes and Walks

Unless indicated otherwise, a Northwest Forest Pass is required to park at trailheads for all of the following hikes and walks. Unless noted, dogs are allowed as long as they're leashed. For the most up-to-date information on conditions, call Glacier Public Service Center at (360) 599–2714 or Mount Baker Ranger District in Sedro-Woolley at (360) 856–5700.

Summer snow at Artist Point

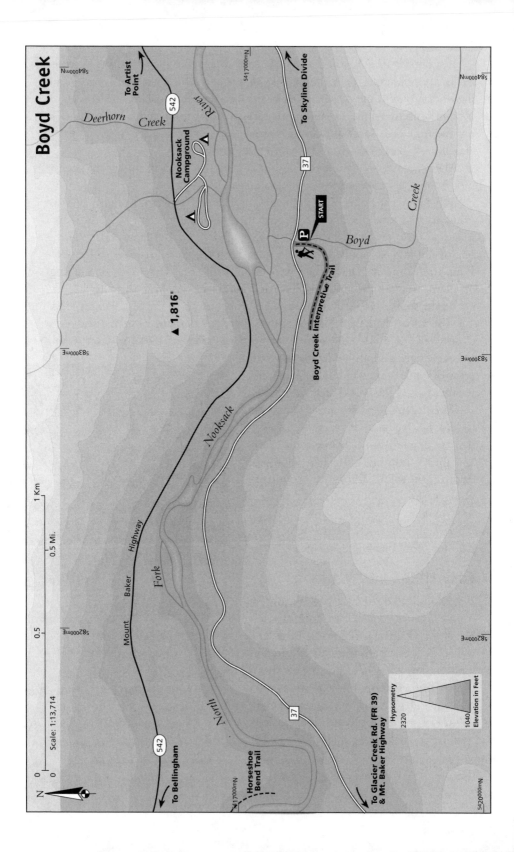

Boyd Creek

Scale: 1:13,714

N

0   0.5   1 Km
0   0.5 Mi.

To Bellingham

To Artist Point

542

Deerhorn Creek

Nooksack Campground

▲ 1,816'

River

37

START

P

Boyd Creek Interpretive Trail

To Skyline Divide

Boyd Creek

Mount Baker Highway

North Fork Nooksack

Horseshoe Bend Trail

37

To Glacier Creek Rd. (FR 39)
& Mt. Baker Highway

Hypsometry
2320
1040
Elevation in Feet

5840000mN
5417000mN
583000mE
582000mE
5417000mN
5420000mN

1 Boyd Creek Interpretive Trail

TYPE OF TRAIL: Barrier-free; hikers and walkers only; interpretive signs.

TOTAL DISTANCE: 0.5 mile out-and-back.

TIME REQUIRED: 30 minutes.

DIFFICULTY LEVEL: Easy.

ELEVATION GAIN: 20 feet.

MAPS: Green Trails Mount Baker 13 (trail not shown).

STARTING POINT: Go east on Highway 542 (Mount Baker Highway) to milepost 34.3. Turn right onto Glacier Creek Road and then make a quick left onto Forest Service Road 37. The trailhead is 3.3 miles ahead on the right.

THE HIKE: This relatively new (2000) self-guided interpretive walk follows recently restored Boyd Creek, an important spawning habitat for members of the anadromous world. That's salmon and trout to you and me. Signs along this forested, mostly boardwalk trail detail the life cycles of species such as chinook, pink, and coho salmon, as well as steelhead and cutthroat trout.

From the interpretive sign in the parking lot, follow the wide, hard-packed dirt trail into the woods. Just ahead, reach the creek itself and the first viewing area. If you're lucky, you might be able to observe one of the aforementioned species in various states of spawn.

The trail continues to the right as an elevated boardwalk, mucho shaded and thus primed for moisture. Most likely it'll be slippery, so be careful. Interpretive signs are interspersed the rest of the way, and by the end of the walk, you'll be an expert on the anadromous world.

2 Horseshoe Bend Trail

TYPE OF TRAIL: Hiking only.

TOTAL DISTANCE: About 2.4 miles out-and-back.

TIME REQUIRED: 1 to 2 hours.

DIFFICULTY LEVEL: Easy.

ELEVATION GAIN: 350 feet.

MAPS: Green Trails Mount Baker 13.

STARTING POINT: The pullout parking area and trailhead are on the right side of the road at milepost 35.4 on the Mount Baker Highway, about 2 miles east of Glacier.

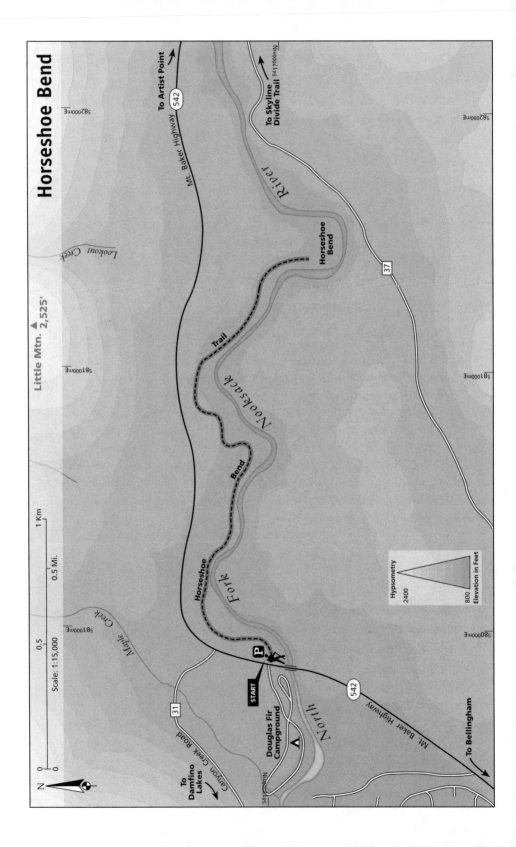

Horseshoe Bend

Little Mtn. ▲ 2,525'

Scale: 1:15,000

To Artist Point

To Skyline
Divide Trail

542

Mt. Baker Highway

Lookout Creek

River

Horseshoe
Bend

37

Nooksack

Trail

Bend

Horseshoe

Fork

Maple Creek

31

Canyon Creek Road

To
Damfino Lakes

North

P

START

Douglas Fir
Campground

542

Mt. Baker Highway

To Bellingham

N

Hypsometry

2400

800

Elevation in Feet

THE HIKE: Most of the area's marquee hikes are higher-elevation affairs, which is great, but they're hikable only in summer and early fall. Here's a gem that's low enough to be passable just about year-round. You'll thrill to the rushing Nooksack River powering its way through everything and anything in its path—house-size boulders, snags, the riverbed, kayakers. In summer this is the put-in spot for several kayaking outfitters. This is the North Fork of the Nooksack River here, and it gets its start from glaciers on the north side of Mount Shuksan.

The mostly gentle riverside trail meanders through a forest of giant moss-hung firs, hemlocks, and cedars that all but block out the rain on those rainy days. This is a great any-time-of-day, any-time-of-year hike that's suitable for the whole family.

First up, head down the wood steps that lead to the river's edge. Follow the trail to the left as it parallels the at-times raging Nooksack squeezing its way through a narrow gorge. In a few hundred yards the trail climbs some steps and enters the deeper and darker woods. After crossing a log bridge—grab hold of those young ones, because it doesn't have a railing—reach a perfectly placed bench at river's edge. If you're not careful, you'll sit here for hours ogling Mother Nature's powerful waterworks. The river seems to explode right before your very eyes. Scan the tamer parts of the river for rock-hopping American dippers, small, gray, sparrow-size birds that dive-bomb the creek for insects. This makes a nice turnaround point if you've got other stops on your schedule.

If you're continuing on, about 0.7 mile from the trailhead, after leaving the river's edge, go right onto a dirt road in a semiopen power line area. The trail gradually returns to river's edge, becoming more overgrown as it does so. At about 1.2 miles, after a steep hillside-hugging stretch, the trail becomes too overgrown to continue without difficulty. Best to turn around here.

3 North Fork Nooksack Research Natural Area

TYPE OF TRAIL: Hiking only.

TOTAL DISTANCE: About 0.5 mile out-and-back.

TIME REQUIRED: 30 minutes.

DIFFICULTY LEVEL: Easy.

ELEVATION GAIN: 30 feet.

MAPS: Green Trails Mount Baker 13, Mount Shuksan 14 (trail not shown).

NOTE: Northwest Forest Pass not required.

STARTING POINT: The unmarked pullout parking area and trailhead are on

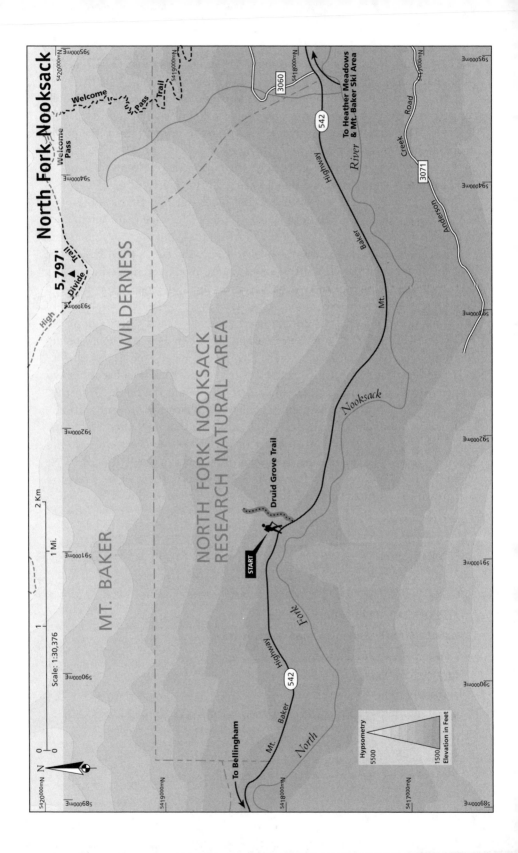

the left (north) side of the Mount Baker Highway at about milepost 43.9. There is another pullout area just east of here, too.

THE HIKE: This is a crane-your-neck-in-wonder walk, an easy I-can't-believe-the-size-of-these-trees jaunt that'll have you snapping off photos at the rate of one a minute. This 1,400-acre roadside forest was set aside in 1937, and without much effort forest lovers can step out of their cars and almost immediately find themselves in a cathedral of 700-plus-year-old Douglas firs, western red cedars, and western hemlocks, many of them 8 to 10 feet in diameter.

Shortly after entering the forest, you notice a large fallen log to your right. Walk for a bit, stopping numerous times to link arms with your partner around a massive hemlock trunk, gawk at the ridiculously high piles of needles at many of the trees' bases (the needles have been falling for centuries, after all), gape at the height of these forest sentinels, and just shake your head in wonder at the forest ecology and nature in general. Look again to the right and note that the first fallen log is still there with you—it's that long. (And you can't help but wonder, if there was no one to hear it, did it make any sound when it fell?)

Massive trees in the North Fork Nooksack Research Natural Area

The trail itself meanders and can be a bit primitive. When trees and branches fall, they tend to stay there. Also, because this is a research area, be especially careful not to take anything more than pictures or to leave anything more than footprints.

Heather Meadows

What follows are some of the easier hikes and walks to be found at the Heather Meadows Area. Many of these trails were built in the late 1920s when the Mount Baker Lodge, a posh 100-room resort, was located here. So there are many short loops that connect back to the main parking lots.

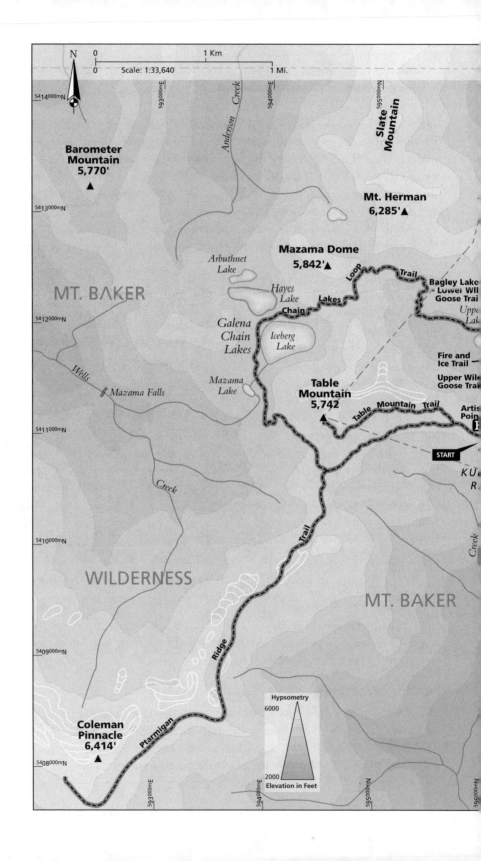

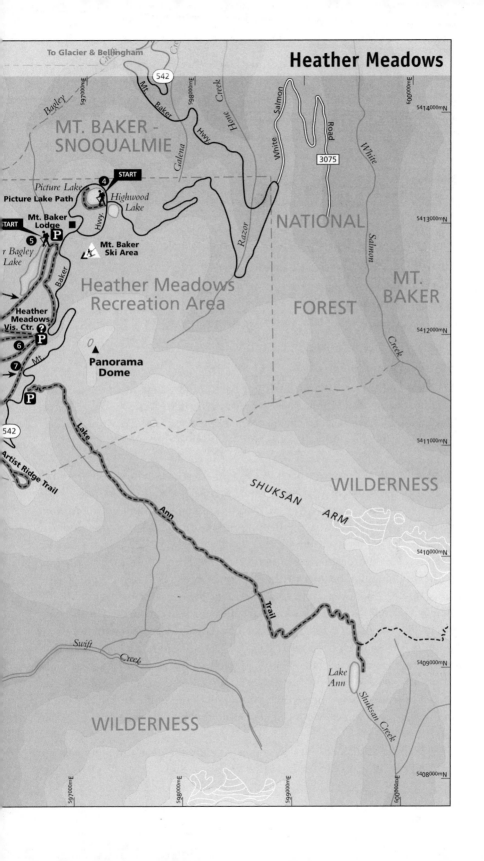

Heather Meadows

To Glacier & Bellingham

MT. BAKER -
SNOQUALMIE

Picture Lake
Picture Lake Path
Highwood
Lake

START

Mt. Baker
Lodge

TART

Bagley
Lake

Mt. Baker
Ski Area

Heather Meadows
Recreation Area

Heather
Meadows
Vis. Ctr.

Panorama
Dome

Artist Ridge Trail

NATIONAL

FOREST

MT.
BAKER

WILDERNESS

SHUKSAN

ARM

Swift Creek

Lake
Ann

Shuksan Creek

WILDERNESS

Lake Ann Trail

597000mE
598000mE
599000mE
600000mE

5414000mN
5413000mN
5412000mN
5411000mN
5410000mN
5409000mN
5408000mN

Call the Glacier Public Service Center (360–599–2714) for the latest conditions and to find out how far the Mount Baker Highway is open. In general the last 3 miles don't open until sometime in July and close in October. Often the road is plowed as far as the Heather Meadows Visitor Center—about a mile past the ski area's upper lodge—for a couple weeks before and after those dates.

4 Picture Lake Path

See map on pages 30–31.

TYPE OF TRAIL: Barrier-free; hiking and walking only.

TOTAL DISTANCE: 0.5 mile out-and-back.

TIME REQUIRED: 30 minutes.

DIFFICULTY LEVEL: Easy.

ELEVATION GAIN: None.

MAPS: Green Trails Mount Shuksan 14.

NOTE: No dogs allowed.

STARTING POINT: Go east on the Mount Baker Highway to milepost 54.1, just below the Mount Baker Ski Area Heather Meadows Day Lodge. You'll have reached the lake when you come to the one-way loop that follows Picture Lake's shoreline. Park on the wide shoulder.

THE HIKE: Even if you've never been to Heather Meadows before, you'll probably experience a sense of déjà vu as soon as you step out of the car. That's because that natural wonder you're probably staring at right now—Mount Shuksan and its mirrored image reflecting in Picture Lake, not to mention the kaleidoscope of colors from the heathers and wildflowers filling in the spaces between—graces more postcards, calendars, and phone books than just about any other mountain. And lots of those photos were taken right from where you're standing. So, note to self: *Don't forget the camera.*

The wheelchair-accessible, pavement-and-boardwalk path around the lake is very family friendly (though dogs aren't allowed) and offers a number of short exploratory offshoot trails as well. Check the trailhead kiosk map to orient yourself. There are picnic tables here, so pack a lunch; a short dock extends partway into the lake for further exploration. Nearby peaks include Mount Herman to the west, flat-topped Table Mountain to the south, and Ruth Mountain to the east, just left of Mount Shuksan and looking like she wants to get in the photo, too.

This hike is a gem, and best yet, because it's so short, you can jump back in the car and continue up the road to other trails.

See map on pages 30–31.

TYPE OF TRAIL: Hiking only.

TOTAL DISTANCE: 1.5-mile loop.

TIME REQUIRED: 1 hour.

DIFFICULTY LEVEL: Easy.

ELEVATION GAIN: 150 feet.

MAPS: Green Trails Mount Shuksan 14.

STARTING POINT: Continue east on the Mount Baker Highway to milepost 55 and the upper parking lot for the Mount Baker Ski Area Heather Meadows Day Lodge. Follow the sign for Bagley Lakes.

THE HIKE: From the parking lot follow the trail sign down into the narrow Bagley Creek gorge, many moons ago the site of a hydroelectric power plant for the long-gone posh resort that was the Mount Baker Lodge. (It burned down in 1931.) With flat-topped Table Mountain looming straight ahead to the south, follow this gentle path as it wends its way alongside lake and creek between Mount Herman on your right and the ski area's Panorama Dome on your left.

Lower Bagley Lake comes first, then the creek, rushing and gushing its way through a boulder-choked gorge. Ooh and ahh at wildflowers and munch on handfuls of blueberries galore (in late summer and early fall) and then, watch your step. You're in a gorge with lots of snowmelt just above lots of water all around, which means lots of mud.

Take note of the columnar andesite on your left. How will you know it? The word *columnar* is the key. About 300,000 years ago, this basin was awash in lava. When it cooled, it did so quickly and formed into very distinct six-sided columns of grayish rock that fit together like pieces in a puzzle. These columnar joints can be seen at places throughout Heather Meadows.

Continuing south, at about 0.7 mile from the trailhead, reach a stone bridge crossing Bagley Creek. Instead of crossing it—it leads to the Chain Lakes Loop Trail (see Hike 16)—go left and climb one of several trails leading to the Heather Meadows Visitor Center. Cross a stretch of flattened andesite that resembles the outside of a giant bowl that's been flipped upside down. To the right, Upper Bagley Lake sits in a large open—and almost always snow-filled—basin below Table Mountain's mighty prow.

Beyond the visitor center find the sign for the Wild Goose Trail and go left through the Austin Pass Picnic Area—or enjoy a picnic, it's up to you—and head north through a mix of heathery meadows and open forest. (The signed

Tomyhoi Peak and Mount Larrabee above Bagley Lake

Fire and Ice Trail for Hike 6 is to the right.) Out of the Bagley Creek gorge, you're treated to views of a host of Cascade peaks from Tomyhoi Peak to Mount Larrabee to Goat Mountain that look close enough to touch but are actually just south of the United States–Canada border. Follow the well-marked trail back to the parking lot where you started.

6 Fire and Ice Trail

See map on pages 30–31.

TYPE OF TRAIL: Barrier-free; hiking and walking only; interpretive signs.

TOTAL DISTANCE: 0.5 mile.

TIME REQUIRED: 30 minutes.

DIFFICULTY LEVEL: Easy.

ELEVATION GAIN: None.

MAPS: Green Trails Mount Shuksan 14.

STARTING POINT: Go east on the Mount Baker Highway to about milepost 55 and the Heather Meadows Visitor Center. The signed trailhead is to the left of the visitor center.

THE HIKE: Short but sweet, this wide, mostly paved and completely easy-to-follow trail winds its way through open meadow and forest populated by ancient hemlocks. But just because they're old, don't expect megagiant tree trunks—they're at 4,400 feet here, and so most of the year they're covered in snow and have a short growing season. (Perhaps that's the secret to staying young-looking—spend most of the year buried under the snow.)

The first half of the half-mile loop is paved; after that, the gravel trail is wide and still easy to follow.

7 Upper Wild Goose Trail

See map on pages 30–31.

TYPE OF TRAIL: Hiking only.

TOTAL DISTANCE: 0.8 mile point-to-point.

TIME REQUIRED: 40 minutes.

DIFFICULTY LEVEL: Moderate.

ELEVATION GAIN: 600 feet.

MAPS: Green Trails Mount Shuksan 14.

STARTING POINT: Go east on the Mount Baker Highway to about mile-post 55 and the Heather Meadows Visitor Center. The signed trailhead is to the left of the parking lot.

THE HIKE: Say you've picnicked a tad too much and you need to work some of it off. This is the hike to do it on. Tell your traveling companions that you'll meet them at Artist Point. While they drive the remaining 2 miles of road switch-backs, you head up this trail, which makes no ifs, ands, or buts about tackling the elevation. The trail, a mix of singletrack, rock steps, and more than likely snow, climbs heathery hillocks and wildflower meadows, sometimes roadside, sometimes not, before opening up just across from the Artist Point parking lot. Sure, it's steep, but it's short, and the alpine views are more than grand the entire way. Best yet, you can bum a ride on the way back down.

8 Artist Ridge Trail

See map on pages 30–31.

TYPE OF TRAIL: Hiking only.

TOTAL DISTANCE: 1 mile out-and-back.

TIME REQUIRED: 45 minutes.

DIFFICULTY LEVEL: Easy.

ELEVATION GAIN: 150 feet.

MAPS: Green Trails Mount Shuksan 14.

STARTING POINT: Go to the end of the road—follow the Mount Baker Highway east for 57 miles to the road-end Artist Point parking lot.

THE HIKE: If you're pressed for time, make this the one hike you do on your visit to the Mount Baker–Mount Shuksan area. You get the best of everything— countless Cascade peaks, subalpine meadows, snowfields for silly August snow-ball fights, and close-up views of both Mount Baker and Mount Shuksan—with the least amount of effort.

The view from the parking lot itself is awesome, but for more, find the paved trailhead at the southeast corner of the parking lot (Mount Shuksan side) and follow the trail for about 100 yards to a south-facing vista. (In theory the trail has interpretive signs, but either vandals or the 25 feet of snow that falls here each year have done away with them.) Here you're treated to neck-craning views of Mount Baker and its icy, crevasse-riddled glaciers to the south; Baker Lake almost 10,000 feet below at the terminus of countless evergreen folds and ridges; and Mount Shuksan just 4 air miles away.

Artist Ridge and Mount Shuksan

Follow the trail along Kulshan Ridge in Shuksan's direction, stopping as you no doubt will to admire the tiny tarns (ponds) and permanent snowfields with their eerie blue ice, just at the trail's edge. Continue for about a half mile to a rocky area, Huntoon Point, at the ridge's east end. On ultraclear days scan the horizon to the south for Glacier Peak and Mount Rainier, the latter about 150 miles away and the only mountain in the Lower 48 with more snow, ice, and glacier than Mount Baker.

Out-and-back trails can sometimes be a drag, but not this one. On the way back to the trailhead, views of sky-kissing Mount Baker and Table Mountain are awe-inspiring. So are look-sees at Mount Larrabee and Tomyhoi Peak and Yellow Aster Butte and Goat Mountain and the Nooksack Ridge and too many peaks to count.

Day Hikes

The following are longer trails, most of which are 4 to 10 miles round-trip and require 2,000 or more feet of elevation gain. These trails are well marked and easy to follow. However, they can be subject to harsh weather conditions. Blowdown and washout are common and can make trails impassable. For the most up-to-date information on conditions, call the Glacier Public Service Center at (360) 599–2714 or Mount Baker Ranger District in Sedro-Woolley at (360) 856–5700. The Mount Baker–Snoqualmie National Forest Web site (www.fs .fed.us/r6/mbs) is also a good source for trail conditions, though it's still best to call.

Most of the following trails are snow-free enough for hiking from July through October, but always check with a ranger before heading out. In general snow on south-facing trails such as Church Mountain and Hannegan Pass melts out earlier than it does on north-facing slopes such as Skyline Divide and Heliotrope Ridge.

Because these trails are likely to take you to elevations above 5,000 feet, preparation is important. Always carry the ten essentials (map, compass, extra clothing, extra food, water, flashlight or headlamp with extra batteries and bulb, first-aid kit, matches in a waterproof container and fire starter, pocketknife, and sunglasses and sunscreen) and be aware that the weather can change quickly. Bluebird days with the Fahrenheit hitting 70 can turn dark, cold, and windy at an alarming rate. And don't forget what the old salt told me: Above 5,000 feet, snow is possible any day of the year.

Unless indicated otherwise, a Northwest Forest Pass is required to park at the following trailheads. Cost is $5.00 for a daily pass or $30.00 for an annual pass. Passes are available at the Glacier Public Service Center, the Mount Baker Ranger District office in Sedro-Woolley, and numerous outlets in the area. Finally, unless noted, dogs are allowed as long as they're leashed.

9 Heliotrope Ridge Trail

TYPE OF TRAIL: Hiking only.
TOTAL DISTANCE: 6 miles out-and-back.
TIME REQUIRED: 4 hours.
DIFFICULTY LEVEL: Moderate.
ELEVATION GAIN: 1,900 feet.
MAPS: Green Trails Mount Baker 13.

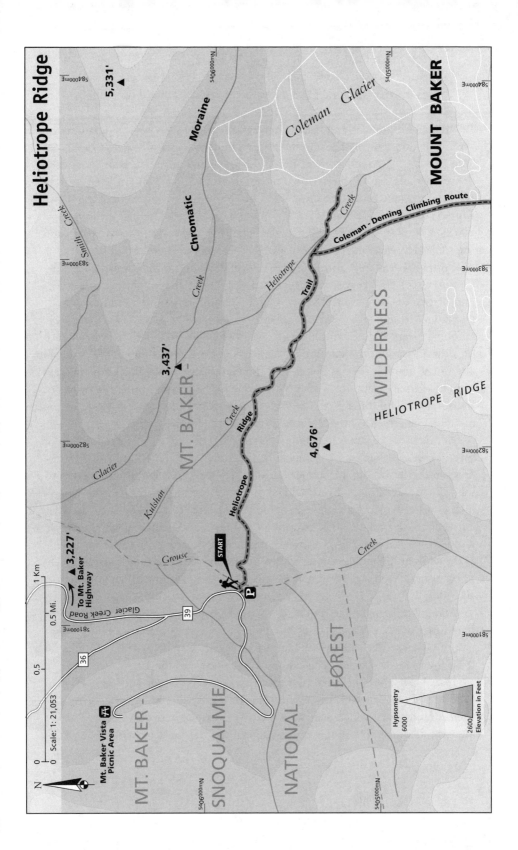

STARTING POINT: Go east on the Mount Baker Highway to milepost 34.3 and signed Glacier Creek Road, also known as Forest Service Road 39. Turn right and continue for 8 miles to a marked trailhead on the left.

THE HIKE: This popular and historic trail offers perhaps the best opportunity on the north side (that is, the Mount Baker Highway side) to experience one of Mount Baker's glaciers up close. In a little less than 3 miles, the trail ends at the toe of the Coleman Glacier, named for Edmund Coleman, who in 1868 became the first person to make it to the summit of Mount Baker. The sight of the snow-white river of ice pouring down the mountainside into a jumble of house-size blocks is truly spectacular, and this trail puts you right there. Those views and the somewhat easy accessibility ensure that on weekends you won't be alone.

From the trailhead, immediately drop down into the forest and cross Grouse Creek via a very stable yet rail-less log bridge that might give you a second or two of pause. Once across, begin climbing on an oft-muddy but well-maintained trail. Take note of the folks you're likely to see wearing plastic climbing boots and carrying oversize packs on their backs—they're headed to or returning from the summit of Mount Baker. Each year about 5,000 climbers attempt to summit Mount Baker, and the Heliotrope Ridge Trail offers access to the Coleman-Deming Glacier Route, one of the two most popular routes to the summit. The other is the Easton Glacier Route on the south side of the mountain, accessed via the Railroad Grade Trail (see Hike 25).

A little more than a mile from the trailhead, you'll need to make the first of several creek crossings. On the upside, they make for some impressive waterfalls; on the downside, during periods of heavy snowmelt higher up the mountain, they're gushing to overflow and you're going to get wet. But hey, that's hiking in the North Cascades. (Why do you think they're called the Cascades, anyway?) Back in the woods, continue climbing via switchbacks, with a couple more creeks and waterfalls thrown in for variety. Be aware that later in the day as the snow at higher elevations has had more time to melt, the creeks are likely to be rushing even more and may possibly be raging torrents. Plan your return accordingly.

About 2 miles from the trailhead, you find a couple of campsites. This is also the former site of the Kulshan Cabin, built in 1925 as a place to spend the night before Glacier Creek Road was built and the only way up here was to hike up from the town of Glacier. The cabin was torn down in the 1980s.

Just ahead, the trail leaves the forest, and Mount Baker and the Coleman Glacier dominate the sky. It's truly awe-inspiring. You'll also reach a fork: Continue straight for about a half mile, getting ever closer to the glacier and the many braids of its meltwater creeks. Listen for the piercing whistles of mar-

Climbers heading for the summit of Mount Baker

mots, which sometimes seem to be crawling on every rock.

If you go right at the fork, you're following the climbers' trail, which after about a half mile of switchbacking takes you to the Hogsback, a popular spot for climbers to camp before attempting the summit. Views here are equally awesome, thus making the climbers' trail a great day-hiking destination in its own right.

Note: With both of these trails, it's imperative that even though the trails lead to a glacier environment, stay off the glaciers themselves unless you are roped up, are carrying an ice ax, and have glacier-travel experience. Glaciers can be deceiving. They may look like harmless snowfields, but in reality, just below the surface might be crevasses 50 to 100 feet deep, and a fall can be deadly.

Once you've had your fill of this alpine splendor, return to the trailhead the same way you came.

10 Skyline Divide Trail

TYPE OF TRAIL: Hiking; open to equestrians from August 1 through October 31; llamas year-round.

TOTAL DISTANCE: 7 miles out-and-back.

TIME REQUIRED: 4 hours.

DIFFICULTY LEVEL: Moderate.

ELEVATION GAIN: 2,100 feet.

MAPS: Green Trails Mount Baker 13.

STARTING POINT: Head east on the Mount Baker Highway to milepost 34.3. Turn right onto Glacier Creek Road and then make a quick left onto Forest Service Road 37, which parallels the Nooksack River for several miles. Follow the sign for the Skyline Divide Trail. The trailhead is 12.7 miles ahead, much of that a tad rough on your car's suspension system.

THE HIKE: Superb high alpine meadows, that's this trail in a nutshell. After switchbacking up a couple forested miles of hemlocks and firs, it's just you and an open ridgetop trail beelining for Mount Baker's north flank, just 5 miles away. Oh, yes, one other thing: splendiferous wildflower meadows, especially in July and August. (And as long as we're being honest, one other thing: bugs. In July and August when the high-elevation snow is still melting out, the mosquitoes and flies can be quite horrendous. Take along an insect repellent that contains DEET and keep moving.)

From the trailhead, climb about 2 miles through second-growth forest, including a brief level stretch that'll make you think the climbing is behind you (not quite). Eventually you'll emerge from the forest onto Skyline Divide, and when you do, there's no mistaking it. You're on top of one of the many high ridges that radiate from Mount Baker like spokes on a wheel, and the views from up here are spectacular to say the least. Baker itself rises surreally high in the sky and seems especially so because the last time you saw it was from down in the Nooksack River valley, many miles away, on the drive in. Walk along the ridge—the grade here is significantly less than the trail's first 2 miles—and the mountain seems to grow and expand before your very eyes. Mount Shuksan is prominent, too, as are unobstructed views of countless peaks (both in the United States and far into Canada), valleys, forests, and the northern reaches of Puget Sound.

Oh, and yes, flowers. The meadows here are arguably the finest for wildflower oglers. You got your lupine, your bistort, your valerian, your potentilla,

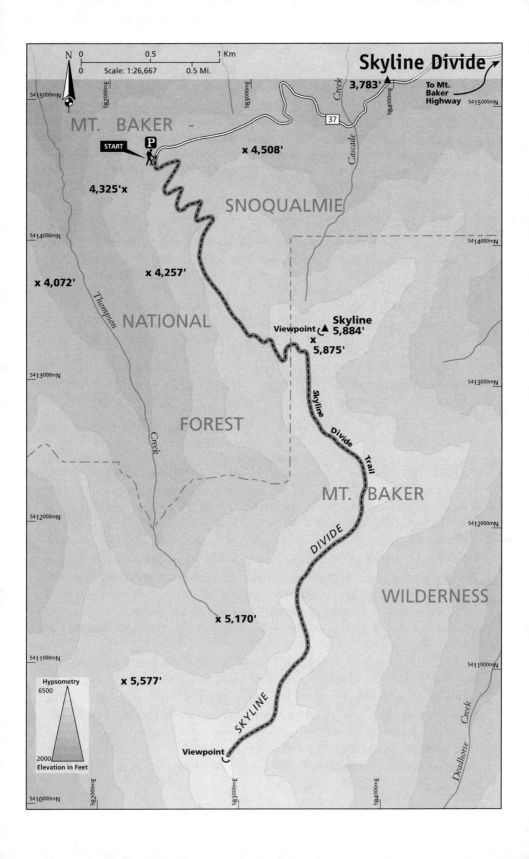

your Indian paintbrush, your phlox, your glacier lily, your partridge foot, your heathers, your five-leaved bramble, your veronica, your et cetera and et alia.

The trail mostly follows the ridgetop, with a number of knolls popping up along the way. Side trails down into basins and up bluffs offer options for exploration, all leading in the general direction of south (toward Mount Baker). Take your pick (you can't go wrong) and really, it's up to your desire, your fitness level, your time crunch, and, of course, the snow level, as to how far you go.

11 Church Mountain Trail

TYPE OF TRAIL: Hiking only.

TOTAL DISTANCE: 8.4 miles out-and-back.

TIME REQUIRED: 6 hours.

DIFFICULTY LEVEL: Difficult.

ELEVATION GAIN: 3,900 feet.

MAPS: Green Trails Mount Baker 13.

STARTING POINT: Go east on the Mount Baker Highway to milepost 38.7 and signed Church Mountain Road. Turn left and follow the gravel, sometimes partially washed-out road for 2.6 miles to the road-end trailhead.

THE HIKE: This relentlessly steep hike climbs about 1,000 feet per mile on its way to a former fire lookout site and the awesome mountain vista that that role implies. As you approach the steeple (for which the mountain earns its name), you'll find plenty of remnants from the old building that was torn down in the 1960s—cable, nails, bits of metal, and what looks like a still-standing outhouse. On the way up, though, you've got plenty of dark forest to switchback up and then its photographic negative—glorious open subalpine meadows awash in wildflowers and views that are simply stunning. Mountains, valleys, and forests on all sides, and to the west northern Puget Sound and the Strait of Georgia where cities such as Bellingham and Vancouver, British Columbia, hang on at water's edge.

After a somewhat gentle half-mile climb up an overgrown logging road—look for lupine and columbine—the trail begins 2 miles of switchbacks while climbing through old-growth forest. You're given time to contemplate these wondrous trees as well as get to know your hiking partners better. A lot better.

At about 2.5 miles, leave the forest for good and enter the big bowl that is the Deerhorn Creek basin. Depending on your visit, you'll be greeted by wildflowers galore, or a big basin full of snow if it's too early in the season, or

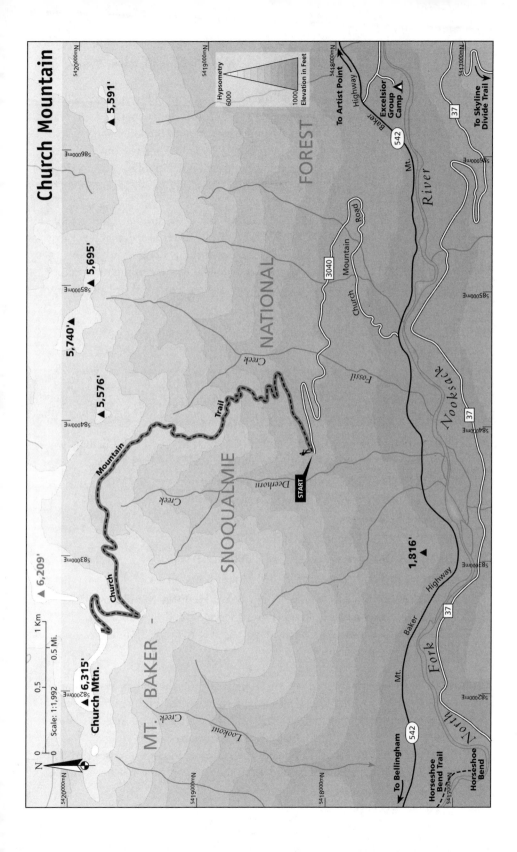

Church Mountain

numerous dry creekbeds if it's too late. In September and October, be sure to pack extra water.

Follow the trail to the west for a little more than a mile, buoyed as you'll be by the increasingly grand views opening to the south the farther you go. The North Fork of the Nooksack River, Mount Baker, Mount Shuksan, and on clear days Mount Rainier are yours for the picking. About 3.7 miles from the trailhead, you'll reach a fork that offers you a choice: go left and follow a steep ridge spine to the top, or go right and take a more leisurely switchback approach. Both lead to the same place.

In about a half mile, reach the rocky bump that is the summit, site of a former lookout cabin built in the late 1920s. Be careful here, as the final few yards feel a bit exposed. Stop just short of the top for the obligatory person-in-outhouse photo. The top makes a great spot for lunch, not to mention taking out your map and spinning round and round as you figure out just how many peaks you can name.

Return the same way.

12 Damfino Lakes–Excelsior Mountain–High Divide Trails

TYPE OF TRAIL: Hiking only on Damfino Lakes Trail; horses and llamas allowed on Excelsior Pass, High Divide, and Welcome Pass Trails.

TOTAL DISTANCE: Varies, from less than 2 miles to almost 20. With two cars, it's possible to make this a point-to-point hike.

TIME REQUIRED: Varies.

DIFFICULTY LEVEL: Moderate to difficult.

ELEVATION GAIN: Varies, from 250 to 3,500 feet.

MAPS: Green Trails Mount Baker 13, Mount Shuksan 14.

STARTING POINT: Go east on the Mount Baker Highway to milepost 35.4 and signed Canyon Creek Road (Forest Service Road 31). Turn left and follow the winding, part-paved, part-gravel road for 15 miles to the road-end parking lot.

THE HIKE: Because it's located on the north side of the ridge, this popular Canyon Creek Road–Damfino Lakes access route to the high country usually melts out a few weeks later than nearby south-facing trails (one reason to consider the options listed after the main trail description).

From the Damfino Lakes Trailhead, the gently graded trail passes through old clear-cut and maturing forest and after about a half mile reaches a signed

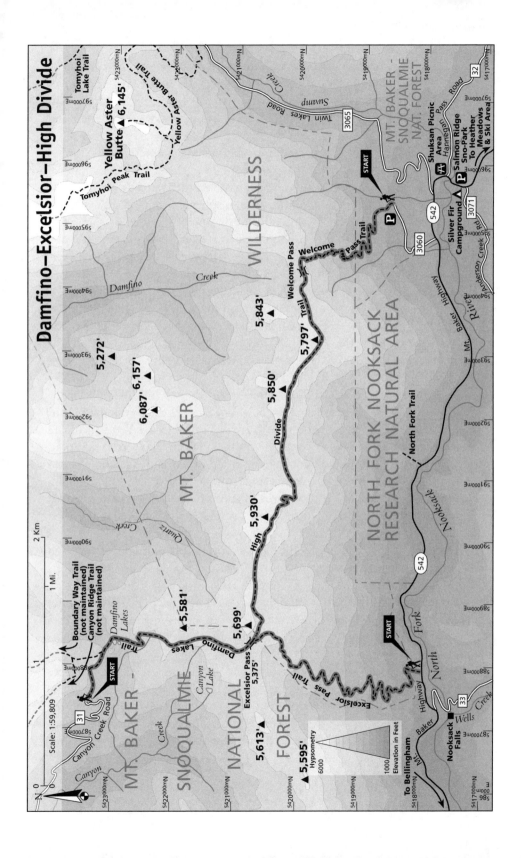

intersection. Go straight and in no time at all reach the tiny, potentially buggy ponds called Damfino Lakes. If it's not too buggy, this area makes a good picnic spot and turnaround point for families with small kids. But if it's the high country you're here for, follow the puncheon bridge walkway to the left and reenter the forest.

Climb fairly steadily for a little more than a mile and, at about 2.2 miles from the trailhead, reach an expansive open meadow. Depending on the time of year, this meadow can be covered in snow; streaked with the reds, purples, yellows, and blues of countless wildflowers and heathers; or some combination of the two. Excelsior Pass, the skyline ridge to the south, is about three-quarters of a mile ahead and doesn't require too strenuous of a climb. And even if it did, the ridgetop views of Mount Baker looming high over the Nooksack River valley, not to mention Mount Shuksan and a hundred other Cascade peaks that are visible (including Mount Rainier when clouds permit), are more than worth it.

If after reaching Excelsior Pass, you're up for even better views, take the obvious trail spur to the east that climbs 400 feet in about a quarter mile to the top of Excelsior Peak, the site of a former fire lookout cabin. The 360-degree mountain views include the aforementioned Cascades peaks as well as countless British Columbian ones including the Coast and Cheam Ranges.

At Excelsior Pass a signed intersection points the way to the High Divide Trail, which follows the gentle ups and downs of High Divide, a wonderful subalpine ridge that heads west for almost 5 miles to Welcome Pass. Subalpine means mostly meadow—so the views from this 5,200- to 5,800-foot (elevation) ridge are stunning—with just enough trees to add variety and, thankfully, shield against the weather if you decide to camp. Any number of knolls and saddles along the ridge make for good turnaround spots. *Caution:* Carry water later in the summer. Once the snow melts, there are few if any water supplies to be found.

Options: If you're interested in less car time and have thighs of steel and the lungs of Lance Armstrong, there are alternative options for gaining Excelsior Mountain, High Divide, and Welcome Pass.

Excelsior Pass Trail, accessed right off the Mount Baker Highway at milepost 41.2, climbs 4,000 feet in 4.2 miles (one way) on its way to Excelsior Pass via a series of seemingly endless switchbacks. All but the last mile is in deep forest.

Welcome Pass Trail, though shorter (2.5 miles one way), is even steeper than the Excelsior Pass Trail, climbing 3,000 feet on the way to Welcome Pass, at the east end of the High Divide Trail. To get to this trail, head east on the Mount Baker Highway to milepost 45.9. Turn left on easy-to-miss and kind of rough Forest Service Road 3060 and continue for about three-quarters of a mile to the road-end trailhead.

If you have at least two cars and are interested in making this a point-to-point day hike, consider parking one car at the Damfino Lakes Trailhead and another at either the Excelsior Pass or Welcome Pass Trailheads. For more climbing than descending, start hiking at Excelsior or Welcome Trailheads.

For High Divide but no Damfino Lakes, park at Excelsior and Welcome Trailheads. For more climbing than descending, start at Excelsior.

13 Yellow Aster Butte–Tomyhoi Lake Trails

TYPE OF TRAIL: Hiking only.

TOTAL DISTANCE: 7 miles out-and-back to Yellow Aster Butte; 8 miles out-and-back to Tomyhoi Lake.

TIME REQUIRED: 4 hours for Yellow Aster Butte; 6 hours for Tomyhoi Lake.

DIFFICULTY LEVEL: Difficult.

ELEVATION GAIN: 2,500 feet for Yellow Aster Butte; 3,500 feet for Tomyhoi Lake.

MAPS: Green Trails Mount Shuksan 14.

STARTING POINT: Go east on the Mount Baker Highway to milepost 46.3 and Twin Lakes Road (Forest Service Road 3065), just past the Department of Transportation maintenance facility. Turn left onto Twin Lakes Road and continue for 4.5 miles to the obvious trailhead.

THE HIKE: This trailhead accesses two trails that probably couldn't be more different. Like it sounds, Yellow Aster Butte is a high rocky outcrop affording 360-degree manna-from-heaven mountain views and flanked by wildflower meadows liberally sprinkled with yellow asters (which aren't actually asters but rather daisies). Tomyhoi Lake, on the other hand, is at the bottom of a wooded valley between two mountains.

If you're a mountain-vista lover, head for Yellow Aster Butte; if you want to fish or camp by a peaceful mountain lake, head for Tomyhoi Lake. Both destinations share the same trail for the first 1.5 miles. From the trailhead, start by switchbacking somewhat steeply up through forest and meadow on a trail built in the early 1900s by miners working claims in the area for the Gold Run Mining Company. (Not a whole lot was ever found.)

About 1.5 miles from the trailhead, after entering an open meadowy bowl, reach a signed junction, where you're given the choice of heading to the right for the lake or to the left for the butte.

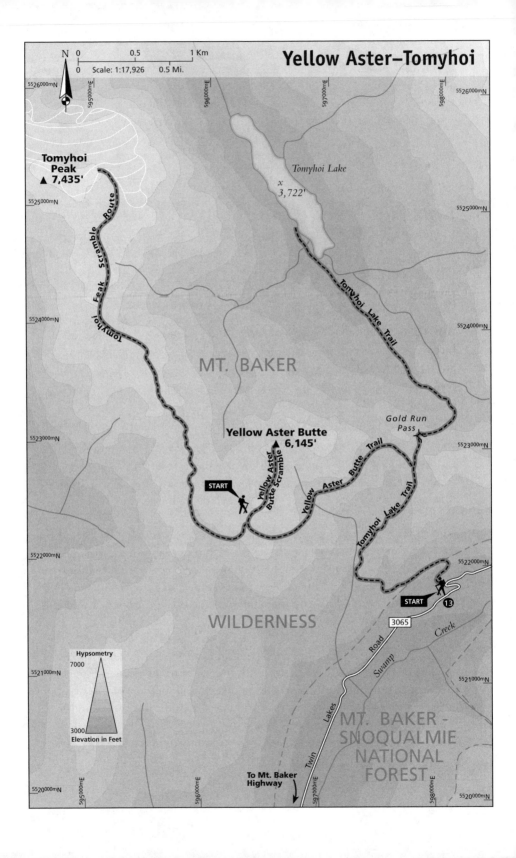

To get to Yellow Aster Butte, contour around the bowl. As you begin to head south, big-time mountain views open up, including Mounts Baker and Shuksan, and just across the Swamp Creek Valley (the one you climbed when you drove Twin Lakes Road), Goat Mountain looking close enough to touch.

Resume climbing along the south-facing slopes in and out of drainages and across the occasional rock garden, until about 3 miles from the trailhead—when you're heading almost due west—you come to a fork in the trail near the rim of a basin. To get to the top of Yellow Aster Butte, go right and climb steeply, gaining 400 feet of elevation in about a half mile. Views from the wide, flat butte are superb—mountains as far away as Mount Rainier to the south, as close as rust-colored Mount Larrabee to the northeast, and everything in between. Tomyhoi Peak, a popular climbing peak, is prominent to the northwest.

Yellow Aster Meadows is below and to the west. To get to the meadows, return to the fork right before the last steep push to the top of Yellow Aster Butte and go left, dropping fairly quickly. Some rocks here in the meadows are more than one billion years old and are among the oldest in the Cascades. In recent centuries glaciers have gouged out numerous small lakes in these meadows. And over the last century, miners practicing leave-as-many-traces-as-you-want wilderness ethics have left an assortment of twisted and rusted mining equipment. Ironically, now that the stuff's been here a while, it's considered historic, and taking any of it is prohibited.

To get to Tomyhoi Lake, continue straight at the fork that's 1.5 miles from the trailhead. Just a couple hundred yards ahead you'll reach Gold Run Pass, where close-up views of Mount Larrabee and the border peaks (American Border Peak and Canadian Border Peak) just 3 miles away will leave you awestruck. (This area actually makes a nice picnic spot or turnaround point if you're pressed for time.) To head to the lake, descend quickly, then more moderately, following the trail as it drops into the forested valley between Yellow Aster Butte and Mount Larrabee.

Try not to let the following thoughts enter your mind: (1) You're losing just about every one of the 1,800 feet of elevation that you gained to get from the trailhead to Gold Run Pass; and (2) you're going to have to gain back every foot of elevation that you're now losing on your way from Gold Run Pass to the lake. These, by the way, are two good reasons to consider making this an overnighter. Reach the lake about 4 miles from the trailhead. Because of avalanche debris, the last stretch of trail just before the lake can be hard to follow.

14 Winchester Mountain Lookout–High Pass Trails

TYPE OF TRAIL: Hiking only.

TOTAL DISTANCE: 3.2 miles out-and-back to Winchester Mountain Lookout; 4 miles out-and-back for High Pass.

TIME REQUIRED: 2 hours for Winchester Mountain; 2½ hours for High Pass.

DIFFICULTY LEVEL: Moderate.

ELEVATION GAIN: 1,350 feet for Winchester Mountain; 1,400 feet for High Pass.

MAPS: Green Trails Mount Shuksan 14.

STARTING POINT: Go east on the Mount Baker Highway to milepost 46.3 and Twin Lakes Road (Forest Service Road 3065), just past the Department of Transportation maintenance facility. Turn left onto Twin Lakes Road and continue for 7 miles to the trailhead between Twin Lakes.

THE HIKE: The Winchester Mountain Lookout, a 14-foot by 14-foot wood cabin built atop a 6,500-foot peak in 1935, is the most easily reached fire lookout in the North Cascades. The trail is less than 2 miles long (one way), and in fact, from the parking lot, if you crane your neck way back, you can look up and see the flagpole atop the cabin. However, there is a catch.

The last 2.5 miles of Twin Lakes Road are not maintained, extremely rough, and only getting worse. Many visitors who don't wish to put their vehicle's suspension system through such peril (or suffer the slight concussion that comes from driving this stretch) park at the Yellow Aster Butte Trailhead and hike the last 2.5 miles of the road, which gains 1,600 feet. The High Pass Trail, which leads to high alpine meadows and stunning views of Mount Larrabee and the border peaks, shares the same trailhead.

Find the trailhead on the west side of the lakes, and begin switchbacking gently across a steep slope ablaze with flowers or heather depending on what month you're here. Even from here, the scenery goes up to an eleven with peaks above and all around including the alliterative Big Bosom Buttes. Below, check out the jewel-like Twin Lakes, often frozen over into August. Across the lake is the Lone Jack Mine, the site of the area's biggest gold strike and cause of the 1898 gold rush. Even today, the mine is still worked from time to time.

About a quarter mile from the trailhead, continue straight at the fork and after climbing steadily for a little more than a mile—traversing one or more snow crossings in the process—reach the lookout. The spectacular mountain

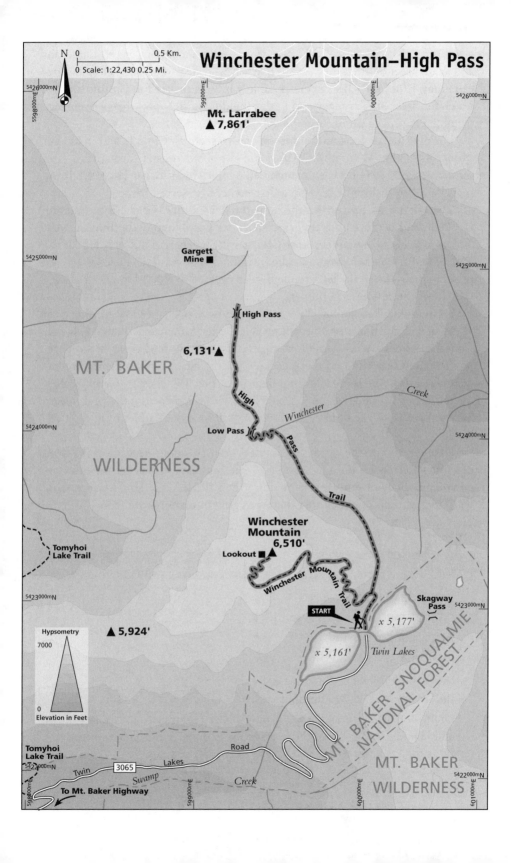

views offer that "sea of peaks" effect wherein the mountains are so numerous and in all directions that they appear like waves—one row of peaks after another extending to infinity. It's understandable why this makes for a primo spot to watch for fires, which rangers did in this building until 1966, when surveillance from planes proved more feasible.

Luckily, unlike lookout cabins on peaks such as Church and Excelsior Mountains, the Winchester Mountain Lookout wasn't dismantled and removed. Since 1982 it's been maintained by the Mount Baker Hiker Club and is available for overnight stays on a first-come, first-served basis.

The High Pass Trail shares the same trailhead as the Winchester Mountain Lookout, and because both trails are short, it's possible to do both in one day. The trail leads to alpine meadows (aburst with blueberries in early fall) at the foot of a rust-colored pyramid called Mount Larrabee. The Pleiades are the peaks to the right; to the left are the border peaks, two 8,000-footers straddling the United States-Canada border.

From the trailhead follow the trail as it climbs an open meadow, turning right at the signed junction with the trail to Winchester Mountain. About a half mile from the trailhead, reach a saddle that offers the first big-time views to the afore-mentioned meadow and northern peaks. Over the next 1.5 miles the trail roller-coasters a bit, dropping down a tad into the Winchester Creek Valley, switchbacking up a talus slope to Low Pass where views open to the west toward Yellow Aster Butte, and finally reaching High Pass about 2 miles from the trail-head.

Hike for a bit on the various exploratory trails; heading west across the front of Mount Larrabee, you're likely to come across rusty remains of the old Gar-gett mine. They're remnants of a time when these mountains were crawlin' with men who had a hunch that there was gold in them thar hills.

15 Hannegan Pass Trail

TYPE OF TRAIL: Hiking only.

TOTAL DISTANCE: 8 miles out-and-back.

TIME REQUIRED: 5 hours.

DIFFICULTY LEVEL: Moderate.

ELEVATION GAIN: 2,000 feet.

MAPS: Green Trails Mount Shuksan 14.

STARTING POINT: Go east on the Mount Baker Highway to milepost 46.5 and Hannegan Pass Road (Forest Service Road 32). Turn left and con-tinue for 1.3 miles to a fork. Go left; the road-end trailhead is 4 miles ahead.

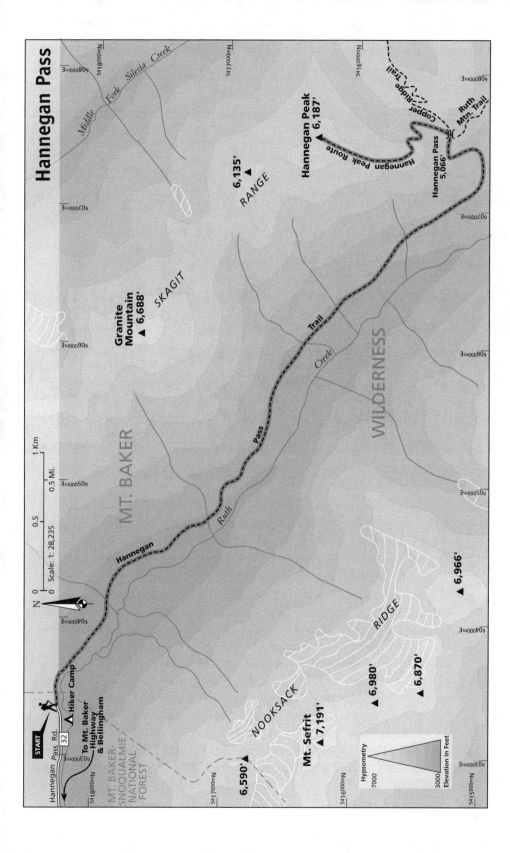

Hannegan Pass

Heather against the backdrop of the Nooksack Ridge

THE HIKE: One of the first trails on the north side to melt out, the Hannegan Pass Trail is also largely in the open. It passes only briefly through stretches of forest, thus offering superb mountain and waterfall views almost the entire way. Plus, except for the last three-quarters of a mile right before the pass, the grade is fairly gentle the whole way.

A couple cautions are in order, however. While the snow here melts out sooner than on other trails, early in the hiking season creeks are covered by snow bridges that, as the season goes on, weaken as they melt. Be sure to test snow bridges before crossing them. Also, the Forest Service's trail conditions report almost always warns of taking bear precautions near the Hannegan Camp area. (That said, I personally have never seen bears on this trail.)

From the trailhead map kiosk, follow the trail through mostly open meadow just below the looming massif of Granite Mountain on your left. In the valley to your right is Ruth Creek all agurgle, and on the other side of that, the awesome Nooksack Ridge. Count the seemingly countless waterfalls streaming down the ridge, like spigots that Mother Nature forgot to turn off. With your eye, follow Ruth Creek as far east as you can, and at the head of the valley, you'll see frosty-white Ruth Mountain, a 7,000-foot mountain complete with its own small glacier. (It's a fun, mostly nontechnical climb.)

You'll pass in and out of the forest—Ruth Mountain a little bigger and the Nooksack Ridge a little more dramatic each time you emerge from the trees—until at about 3.2 miles from the trailhead, you reach the elevation-gobbling switchbacks. Pass signed Hannegan Camp in about a half mile, and at 4 miles reach Hannegan Pass.

If you're in the mood for a quad buster, follow the signed trail north to the top of Hannegan Peak. You might be tired by the time you reach the top of this 1.2-mile-long, 1,100 feet of elevation-chomping expressway to the summit, but you won't be sorry. The views from the top surpass all superlatives. You feel like you're in the middle of the North Cascades here. Mount Shuksan and Mount Baker, while certainly prominent, are just players in a mountain drama that extends far into British Columbia.

Heather Meadows

The following are day hikes in the Heather Meadows Area. Snow lingers long at this elevation, and because each of these hikes starts at 4,400 feet and higher, it's a good idea to call the Glacier Public Service Center (360–599–2714) for the latest conditions and to find out how far the Mount Baker Highway is open.

16 Chain Lakes Loop Trail

See map on pages 58–59.

TYPE OF TRAIL: Hiking only.

TOTAL DISTANCE: 7-mile loop.

TIME REQUIRED: 4 hours.

DIFFICULTY LEVEL: Difficult.

ELEVATION GAIN: 1,850 feet.

MAPS: Green Trails Mount Shuksan 14.

STARTING POINT: Go east on the Mount Baker Highway to about mile-post 55 and the Heather Meadows Visitor Center. The signed trailhead is to the left of the parking lot.

THE HIKE: Looped day hikes—always a plus because every step is one through new territory—are hard to come by in the Mount Baker–Mount Shuksan area, which is probably why the Chain Lakes Loop is so popular. That and the

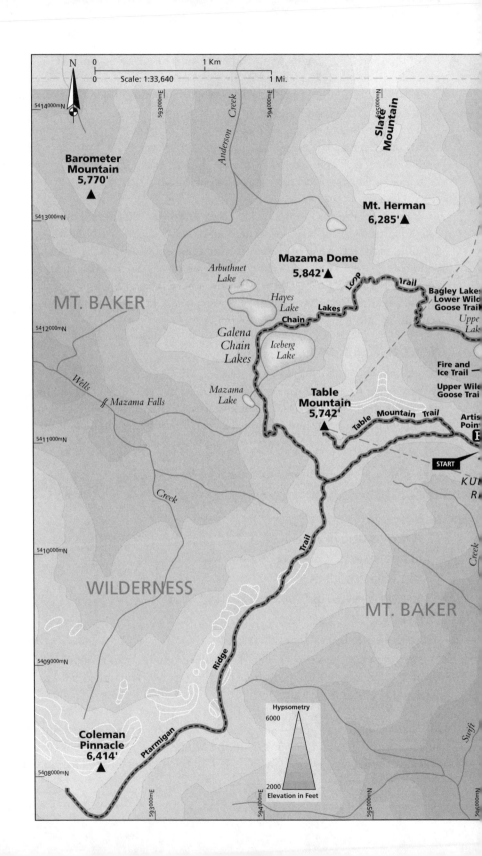

N

0   1 Km

0   Scale: 1:33,640   1 Mi.

5414000mN

593000mE

594000mN

Anderson Creek

Slate Mountain

6285000mN

Barometer Mountain 5,770' ▲

5413000mN

Mt. Herman 6,285'▲

Mazama Dome 5,842'▲

Arbuthnet Lake

Loop

Trail

MT. BAKER

Hayes Lake

Lakes

Bagley Lakes Lower Wild Goose Trail

5412000mN

Chain

Galena Chain Lakes

Iceberg Lake

Uppe Lak

Fire and Ice Trail

Mazama Lake

Table Mountain 5,742'

Upper Wild Goose Trai

ff Mazama Falls

Wells

Table   Mountain   Trail

Artis Poin

5411000mN

▲

START

KU R

Creek

5410000mN

Trail

Creek

WILDERNESS

Ridge

MT. BAKER

5409000mN

Hypsometry

6000

Coleman Pinnacle 6,414'

Ptarmigan

5408000mN

▲

2000

Elevation in Feet

593000mE

594000mE

595000mN

596000mN

Swift

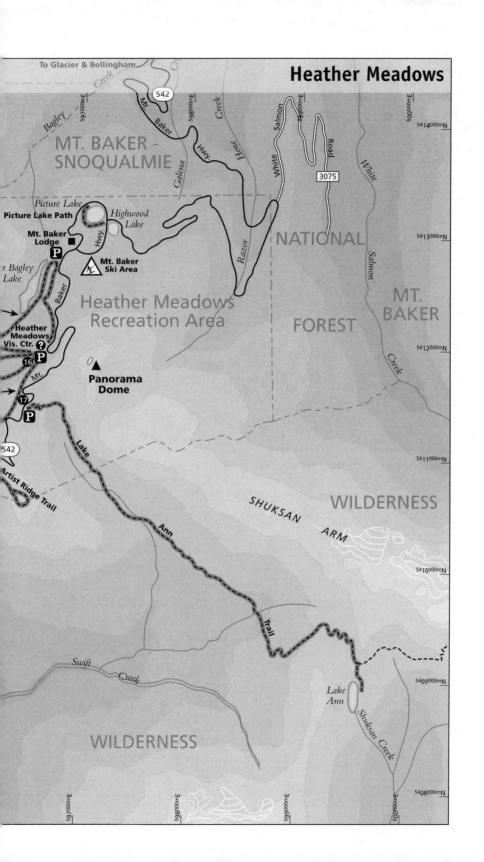

Table Mountain and Herman Saddle above the Bagley Lakes

scenery, which includes a little bit of everything that you could want in a North Cascades hike.

There are the titular big mountains, of course, plus wildflower and blueberry meadows, scree (loose rock) slopes, lava cliffs, a high-alpine traverse with expansive unobstructed Cascade views and permanent snowfields, not to mention the peaceful, contemplative kettle lakes for which the trail is named. In the too-short era of the Mount Baker Lodge (1927–1931), pack horses would follow this loop as they took visitors on fishing excursions to the Chain Lakes.

Oh, yes, this loop has one more thing: a steep climb to start out with—a mix of trail and stone steps that gains about 600 feet in the first 0.8 mile to Artist Point—but once you've finished that, most of the really steep climbing is behind you. (Of course if you have two cars, you can do away with this steep part by parking one car at the Heather Meadows Visitor Center and the other at Artist Point; start the hike at Artist Point and finish it at the visitor center.)

The following description assumes you only have one car and that you'll be starting and finishing at the Heather Meadows Visitor Center. From the visitor center, find the Upper Wild Goose Trail (see Hike 7) and follow as it climbs seemingly straight up the mountainside to Artist Point, roughly paralleling the road as it does so. Very roughly. The road, which switchbacks several times on its way to the road-end parking lot, takes 2 miles to get there; this trail gets to the same place in about three-quarters of a mile, so you know parts of it are going to be steep.

At Artist Point proceed across the parking lot to the southwest (toward Mount Baker) and look for the signed Chain Lakes–Ptarmigan Ridge Trailhead. After a short scoot across a rocky subalpine meadow, follow the mostly level trail as it traverses the base of the prominent, flat-topped butte aptly named Table Mountain. Get used to this butte; you'll be hiking alongside it for much of the day.

Mount Baker looms large and seems to rise and dominate even more of the sky with every step. The shark fin along the ridge to the south, Ptarmigan Ridge, is the Coleman Pinnacle and shows up in the movie, *The Deer Hunter*, which, for some reason, shot many of its exterior scenes of western Pennsylvania here. At about 2 miles from the Heather Meadows Visitor Center, you reach the intersection with the Ptarmigan Ridge Trail (see Hike 19). Go right and head down into the forested lakes area.

In about a mile the trail snakes through a magical meadow of heather and blueberries and four chilly alpine lakes—Mazama, Iceberg, Hayes, and Arbuthnet—some of which the trail passes close enough for skipping stones, others of which you only look down on from above. Aptly named Iceberg Lake, directly below towering Table Mountain, almost always has huge blocks of snow floating in it, even late in the warmest of summers.

Various exploratory trails head off in all directions and make for some wonderful wandering opportunities, but please be careful to stay on the trails—the growing season is short up here and off-trail footprints cause long-term plant damage and disturb animals. Note the campsites (small signs with a tent on them) and keep this place in mind if you're looking for a sublime, not-too-hard-to-get-to backcountry camping trip.

To continue the loop follow the main trail as it climbs steadily for about a mile to Herman Saddle. How will you know when you've reached the saddle? Well, it'll seem like a whole new world has been opened up to you, one dominated by spectacular head-on views of Mount Shuksan. In the expansive valley below is Upper Bagley Lake and just above that the Heather Meadows Visitor Center, where you parked. It's about 1.5 miles away, almost all of it downhill, but because much of it is on talus slope, watch your footing; it can be slippery.

After crossing a stone bridge at the bottom of the basin, complete the loop by making the short climb up a rocky meadow to the visitor center.

Options: If you don't want to make a loop but still want to visit the Chain Lakes, you have a couple of out-and-back choices.

From Heather Meadows Visitor Center, cross the aforementioned stone bridge and follow the trail up the slope to Herman Saddle. The lakes are about a mile down the other side of the slope. Return the way you came for a round-trip distance of about 5 miles with 1,700 feet of elevation gain.

From Artist Point, follow the foregoing loop description from Artist Point to the Ptarmigan Ridge Trail intersection and down to the lakes on the other side of Table Mountain. Return the way you came for a round-trip distance of 4 miles with 600 feet of elevation gain.

17 Lake Ann Trail

See map on pages 58–59.

TYPE OF TRAIL: Hiking only.

TOTAL DISTANCE: 8.2 miles out-and-back.

TIME REQUIRED: 6 hours.

DIFFICULTY LEVEL: Moderate.

ELEVATION GAIN: 1,800 feet.

MAPS: Green Trails Mount Shuksan 14.

STARTING POINT: Go east on the Mount Baker Highway for 56 miles to the Lake Ann Trailhead, less than a mile above the Heather Meadows Visitor Center.

THE HIKE: If it's an up-close-and-personal audience with Mount Shuksan that you want, the Lake Ann Trail is the one for you. After 4 miles or so of ups and downs, you'll find yourself beside an otherworldly alpine lake of azure blue, staring almost straight up at hanging glaciers thousands of feet overhead. If the Picture Lake view of Mount Shuksan inspires you (the view that graces countless calendars), this view is one that'll stay with you for the rest of your life.

From the trailhead, the first thing you'll notice is that, as opposed to many hikes that start with a forested climb, this one starts with a wooded descent—about 600 feet worth over the first mile (which means, you're right, you'll have those 600 feet to climb on the way back) as you drop into the Swift Creek basin. That's Shuksan Arm, the high ridge to your left, but most likely you'll find yourself staring straight ahead at Mount Shuksan, which seems to draw you closer and closer through this mostly open but likely damp, heathery meadow. Artist Ridge (see Hike 8) is above to the right, its face likely splashed with snow patches or small waterfalls or both.

Take note of folks with big packs—Lake Ann is a popular backcountry camping destination, and the trail offers access to the Fisher Chimneys climbing route to Mount Shuksan's summit. Take note, too, of that rumbling sound from time to time—that's the sound of huge chunks of ice breaking off glaciers high on the mountain and reverberating in the Swift Creek canyon.

Continue along a flat to gently descending grade—entering forest along the way—until, at about 2.5 miles from the trailhead, you reach Swift Creek. More than 200 million years of geologic history come crashing together near this spot, making it a favorite among rock hounds. There are phyllites and greenschists that began as ocean floor 150 million years ago and make up the bulk of the Mount Shuksan massif. Shuksan Arm is underlain by a ridge of 225-million-year-old sedimentary rock, and thrusts of granite from just 2 million years ago intrude on the older rock wherever they have a chance.

After crossing Swift Creek you immediately begin gaining back all that elevation you lost at the beginning of this trail—about 900 feet over the next 1.5 miles, much of it through some of those granite slabs and boulders—to the saddle above the lake. Mount Shuksan's Upper and Lower Curtis Glaciers are big and grand here, and Lake Ann, likely snow-choked long into summer, is below.

Follow the trail down and to the left of the lake and find a pleasant spot for a picnic or a nap. If your desire is for even more up close face time with Mount Shuksan, proceed from the saddle above the lake northeast along the climbers' trail, a somewhat rugged path that climbs fairly steeply for about three-quarters of a mile—entering North Cascades National Park as it does—until you're within spitting distance of the Lower Curtis Glacier.

18 Table Mountain

See map on pages 58–59.

TYPE OF TRAIL: Hiking only.

TOTAL DISTANCE: 2.5 miles out-and-back.

TIME REQUIRED: 2 hours.

DIFFICULTY LEVEL: Moderate.

ELEVATION GAIN: 600 feet.

MAPS: Green Trails Mount Shuksan 14.

NOTE: No dogs allowed.

STARTING POINT: Go to the end of the road—follow the Mount Baker Highway east for 57 miles to the road-end Artist Point parking lot.

Table Mountain cairns framing Mount Shuksan

THE HIKE: This trail to the expansive summit of flat-topped Table Mountain is one that people who live here take out-of-town visitors on to give them a taste of what the North Cascades are truly like—which is one reason you'll never feel lonely here. The crowds, oftentimes busloads of them, love this trail, so try to make it here during the week or superearly or toward sunset on weekends when photographic opportunities can be sublime.

The short, steep trail to the top has been blasted out of an almost vertical lava wall, and while it gets you to the top in a hurry (in about a half mile), it can feel a bit exposed. Small children or those who've done most of their sightseeing through car windows might not feel too comfortable on these rocky switchbacks. That said, give it a try. The trail is wide, and you can always hug the wall on the way up.

The trail starts at the southwest end of the parking lot; look for the interpretive map kiosk and trail sign. After crossing a rocky meadow for a couple hundred yards, reach the base of Table Mountain and head on up. Be careful not to kick rocks on anyone below you, and if you hear anyone above you yell "Rock!" *don't* look up lest you catch one in the face.

Table Mountain, as you no doubt noticed on the drive up, resembles an anvil—dark and weighty with an almost perfectly flat top. It's actually what remains of a massively thick lava flow that occurred about 300,000 years ago, long before Mount Baker ever existed. Its source was a lava vent believed to be just north of where Mount Baker is today. The steep drop-offs on all sides of the mountain were caused by erosion from streams and glaciers.

After not too many switchbacks, you'll round a bend, reach the top, and that'll be it for the climbing. You're on your own. It's a rocky, heathery, snowy place up top, and it seems that exploratory trails lead off through all of it in all directions. Stay on the trails (it's a short growing season up here) and just lollygag as you bask in mountain views that seem to stretch on to infinity. On a slow pirouette, you'll see Mount Baker, the Picket Range (a rugged range lusted after by hard-core climbers), Mount Shuksan, the Nooksack Ridge, the Bagley Lakes and numerous trails in the valley below, the border peaks (so named because they straddle the United States–Canada border), High Divide and Church Mountain, and back again to the slopes and ridges leading to Baker's icy flanks.

Picnic and photo possibilities are everywhere. Take note of the impressive rock cairns that get higher and more complex throughout the summer. The main trail heads west for about three-quarters of a mile, and you're going to have stretches of permanent snowfield to cross. Be aware that there are steep drop-offs on all sides (one reason pets aren't allowed). Enjoy, and when you've had enough, return the way you came. Though some old maps show one, no trail exists that connects the west side of Table Mountain with the Chain Lakes Trail.

19 Ptarmigan Ridge Trail

TYPE OF TRAIL: Hiking only.

TOTAL DISTANCE: Up to 11 miles out-and-back, depending on the snow level.

TIME REQUIRED: Up to 6 hours, depending on turnaround point.

DIFFICULTY LEVEL: Difficult.

ELEVATION GAIN: Up to 2,200 feet.

MAPS: Green Trails Mount Baker 13, Mount Shuksan 14.

STARTING POINT: Go to the end of the road—follow the Mount Baker Highway east for 57 miles to the road-end Artist Point parking lot.

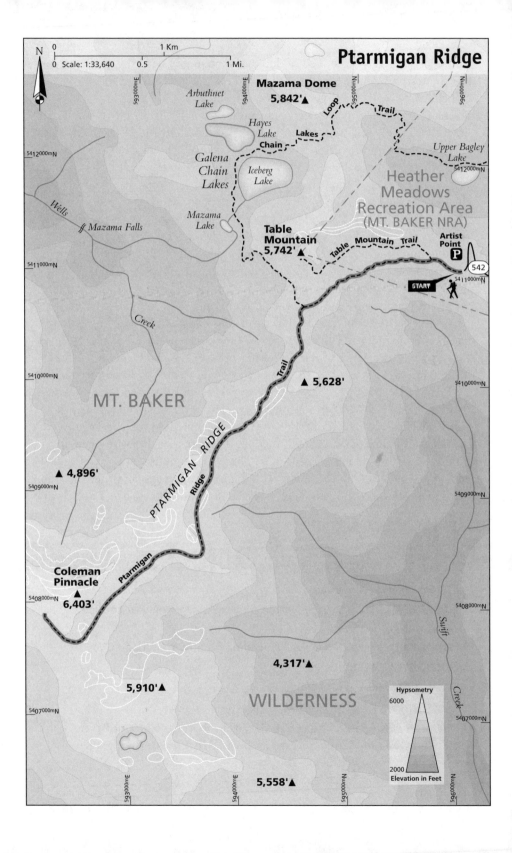

Ptarmigan Ridge

N

0   1 Km
Scale: 1:33,640   0.5   1 Mi.
0

Mazama Dome
5,842' ▲

Arbuthnet Lake

Hayes Lake

Loop   Trail

Galena Chain Lakes

Chain   Lakes

Iceberg Lake

Upper Bagley Lake

Heather
Meadows
Recreation Area
(MT. BAKER NRA)

Wells

Mazama Falls

Mazama Lake

Table Mountain
5,742' ▲

Table   Mountain   Trail

Artist Point
P

542

START

Creek

Trail

▲ **5,628'**

MT. BAKER

PTARMIGAN RIDGE

Ridge

▲ **4,896'**

Coleman Pinnacle
▲
6,403'

Ptarmigan

Swift

4,317' ▲

5,910' ▲

WILDERNESS

5,558' ▲

Creek

Hypsometry
6000

2000
Elevation in Feet

THE HIKE: This high alpine ridge walk is almost entirely above the tree line and thus boasts spectacular unobstructed Cascade views the whole way. On the way out you feel like you're crawling right up the spine of Mount Baker; on the way back you're lured by stunning views of Mount Shuksan, which is in your sight all the way back to Artist Point. If the author had to choose one trail as his personal favorite, this would be it.

That said, this trail also boasts a potential for real danger. It's high, starting at 5,100 feet, and climbs to over 6,400 feet, and the snow melts out later on this trail than on any other in this book. In fact it never completely melts out, and there are a couple stretches where it crosses steeply pitched permanent snowfields. An ice ax, with the ability to use it, is a good idea on this trail.

Then there's the weather. Whiteout conditions are not uncommon, and it's very easy to get lost up here. If the weather makes a turn for the worse, or you find yourself at the edge of a snowfield that's beyond your abilities to negotiate, turn around.

Find the trailhead at the southwest end (Mount Baker side) of the parking lot; look for the interpretive map kiosk and trail sign. Follow the trail as it traverses a mostly level grade below the lava cliffs of flat-topped Table Mountain. After about a mile, go left at the signed intersection; to go right would be to continue around the base of Table Mountain via the Chain Lakes Loop Trail.

Note for the geologically inclined: The Ptarmigan Ridge Trail crosses the remnants of 2.5-mile Kulshan Caldera, the remains of a volcano that blew and filled with ash more than one million years ago. Examples of other noteworthy calderas include Oregon's Mount Mazama, which, after erupting about 7,000 years ago, filled with water to form Crater Lake.

The ridgetop trail is spread out for miles ahead of you at this point, and with good visibility you should immediately be able to tell what the trail conditions are. Is it passable, or are the snow conditions too sketchy to go any farther? (And of course, if visibility is such that you can't see the trail out in front of you, you should probably turn around anyway.) Mount Baker is large and in charge ahead of you; that shark-fin-like peak a couple miles ahead is the Coleman Pinnacle.

Continuing on, after dropping for a short bit, the trail roughens up a tad, then regains the ridge about 2 miles from the trailhead through a short pitch that's likely to be snow-covered. From here the easy-to-follow trail passes through vast meadows, lava fields, talus slopes, and snowfields on a gentle grade, and it's up to you, the weather, and snow level as to how far you continue. The views are beyond stunning from up here, ranging from the rugged Picket Range in the east to northern Puget Sound in the west. And of course Mount Baker, with its crevasse-riddled Rainbow Glacier spilling ever so slowly down its northeast flank, dominates straight ahead to the south.

About 5 miles from Artist Point, look for mountain goats near Camp Kiser, a popular camping spot at the base of the Coleman Pinnacle. Climbers making their way up Baker or the pinnacle often camp here.

Inside the Glacier Public Service Center

Accessible Wilderness

A number of places in the Mount Baker–Mount Shuksan area are barrier-free and thus offer a wilderness experience to everyone. They're accessible not just for wheelchairs but also strollers and other wheeled vehicles. The following is a list of trails, picnic areas, and vista points accessible to all. *(Note:* For information on campgrounds with accessible campsites, see the Camping section.)

Mount Baker Sign, Mount Baker Highway MP 29.1: Though there's no sign, this pullout spot on the right (south) side of the road beckons drivers to stop and admire the first real good views of Mount Baker. Do so here, because even though there's a pullout with an official-looking Mount Baker sign 0.4 mile ahead, over the years the surrounding trees have grown quite tall and now completely block that spot's mountain views.

(In addition, starting at about milepost 37, there are numerous pullout spots with views down to the Nooksack River. Be sure to pull over far enough so that you're not blocking traffic.)

Glacier Public Service Center, Mount Baker Highway MP 33.6: This isn't just a place to ask about the latest trail conditions or purchase a stuffed bear for a loved one. Inside, this seasonal ranger station also has hands-on wheelchair-accessible interpretive displays on Mount Baker and its fauna and flora. Outside you'll find a picnic area and restrooms—and of course that giant slice of Douglas fir tree that dates back some 800 years. The center is open daily from Memorial Day through mid-November and certain weekends the rest of the year.

Boyd Creek Interpretive Trail, Forest Service Road 37, off Mount Baker Highway MP 34.3: This half-mile boardwalk trail, seemingly in the middle of the woods, not only offers a terrific outdoor experience but also features interpretive signage that tells the tale of the local salmon habitat. Because the boardwalk follows the creek, at certain times of the year, visitors can catch a glimpse of salmon and trout in various stages of spawn. Because of the trail's low elevation, it is passable almost year-round. (See Hike 1 for a complete description.)

Mount Baker Viewpoint Picnic Site, at the end of Glacier Creek Road, off Mount Baker Highway MP 34.3: All right, I'll go out on a limb and say it: This is the best view of Mount Baker that you'll get anywhere, and you don't even have to leave your car to get it. But you'll want to. Picnic tables invite you to make an afternoon of it, enjoying the views of Mount Baker's northwest flank. Take binoculars and pick out climbers slogging their way up the Coleman Glacier to the Roman Wall and up to the volcano's summit.

Take the Green Trails map (Mount Baker No. 13) and pick out one geologic feature after another from a forested hillside that climbs to the point where the air is too thin and that forest becomes an open meadow; a meadow that becomes a rocky ridgetop—Chowder Ridge—that leads to Hadley Peak at the head of dark Smith Basin, which leads to the huge, creeping masses of crevasse-riddled ice and snow, the Roosevelt and Coleman Glaciers—the snout of the Roosevelt looks to be sniffing the Glacier Creek valley as it retreats up the mountain—and on to the vanilla-frosting summit of 10,781-foot Mount Baker. Keep your ears open and you'll no doubt hear the "Boom!" of an avalanche or blocks of ice—seracs—crashing atop one another.

To get here, drive 9 miles up Glacier Creek Road to the end. *Note:* Because trees near the picnic site are becoming overgrown, the best, unobstructed views are about a quarter mile *before* the picnic site.

Douglas Fir Campground Picnic Site, Mount Baker Highway MP 35.3: This terrific picnic area is right on one of the most narrow, boulder-choked gorges of the North Fork Nooksack River. Along with the opportunity to enjoy some thrilling white water, it's also a chance to watch white-water kayakers and rafters get tossed around in the water like so many fallen leaves.

Shuksan Picnic Area, off Mount Baker Highway MP 46.5: This riverside site near the intersection of Hannegan Road and the Mount Baker Highway is

Mount Baker's glaciers spilling into the Glacier Creek valley

a little more open than the Douglas Fir site and offers the chance to get a little sun. The North Fork Nooksack River is more mellow this close to its source, with more room to stretch out. *Note:* A Northwest Forest Pass is required to park here. At MP 46.5, turn left onto Hannegan Pass Road; the picnic area is immediately on your right.

Silver Fir Campground Picnic Area, Mount Baker Highway MP 46.9: Just up the road from the Shuksan Picnic Area, this shaded picnic spot features a covered picnic shelter for all-weather use.

Picture Lake, Mount Baker Highway MP 54.1: This is one of the most scenic yet still easy-to-get-to spots in the Northwest. Picture Lake features a pavement-and-boardwalk half-mile trail, picnic tables, and, with Mount Shuksan's picture-perfect reflection in Picture Lake, the likelihood that you'll shoot some of the best photographs you'll ever take in your life. Most years the area is snow-covered from late October to sometime in June. *Note:* No dogs allowed.

Also, a Northwest Forest Pass is required to park here. (See Hike 4 for a complete description.)

Heather Meadows Visitor Center and Austin Pass Picnic Area, Mount Baker Highway MP 55.2: Perched on a rock ledge looking out at the Bagley Lakes basin and flat-topped Table Mountain, this picnic area makes for a super munching spot on a Picture Lake–Artist Point day. (Artist Point is just 2 miles *up* the road and Picture Lake 2 miles *down* the road.) Twenty-plus picnic tables ensure that there's plenty of room for everyone. Visit the Heather Meadows Visitor Center, built in 1940 as a warming hut by the Civilian Conservation Corps, for interpretive displays on the area's flora, fauna, geology, and history. The visitor center is open in summer only.

Also, while here, follow the **Fire and Ice Trail,** a mostly paved path that winds its way through open meadow and stands of ancient hemlocks. Interpretive signs fill you in on what you're seeing. (See Hike 6 for a complete description.) *Note:* A Northwest Forest Pass is required to park here. Most years the area is snow-covered from late October to sometime in June.

Artist Point, Mount Baker Highway MP 57: The end of the Mount Baker Highway offers the best of both worlds—Mount Baker and Mount Shuksan. The views of the two big mountains from the parking lot are out of this world. There are no picnic tables, but the parking lot is big enough that there should be no problem finding a paved, snow-free spot. A short paved trail leads about 100 yards to a slightly higher viewing spot. *Note:* A Northwest Forest Pass is required to park here. Also, most years the area is snow-covered and inaccessible from sometime in October to sometime in July.

Photography

With its glaciated peaks, plunging waterfalls, alpine wildflower meadows, old-growth forest, and raging creeks and rivers, the Mount Baker–Mount Shuksan area is one of the most photogenic in the country. It would seem that it would be pretty much impossible to take a bad photo here, unless you forgot to remove the lens cap from your camera. To that end, what follows is a list of some of the better places to photograph particular features. Remember, the best times to shoot mountain views are usually early morning and early evening when the sunlight often has a golden or reddish tint.

For photographs of:	Go to:
Mount Baker	Mount Baker Viewpoint Picnic Site, Ptarmigan Ridge Trail, Table Mountain
Mount Shuksan	Lake Ann Trail, Artist Ridge Trail, Picture Lake

Mount Shuksan Arm below the icy massif of Mount Shuksan

Waterfalls	Nooksack Falls
Ancient trees	North Fork Nooksack Research Natural Area
Wildflower meadows	Skyline Divide, Yellow Aster Butte
Raging river	Horseshoe Bend Trail
Alpine lakes	Chain Lakes Loop Trail
Cascade "sea of peaks" effect	Winchester Mountain Lookout, Hannegan Peak

Camping

Off the Mount Baker Highway, there are really three ways to go: (1) established Forest Service campgrounds, which offer fire pits, pit toilets, and possibly running water and which take reservations; (2) hiker campsites located at certain trailheads and available on a first-come, first-served basis; and (3) backcountry camping and backpacking, which is free and requires only that you respect the land and your fellow campers.

Developed Campgrounds

The following are developed campgrounds and, unless otherwise noted, are managed by the Forest Service. To reserve a spot at Douglas Fir, Excelsior Group, or Silver Fir Campgrounds, call (877) 444–6777 or visit the Web site at www.reserveusa.com.

Douglas Fir Campground: Located just off the Mount Baker Highway at about milepost 35, this forested twenty-eight-site (tent or trailer) campground is situated right on the North Fork of the Nooksack River (gurgle-gurgle) and makes for great sleeping. Eighteen of the sites can be reserved, the rest are available on a first-come, first-served basis. The campground also features pit toilets, running water, and three wheelchair-accessible sites. This campground is open from May to October. To get here, go east on the Mount Baker Highway to milepost 35.3. The campground is on the left, just past a Nooksack River bridge and across the road from the Horseshoe Bend Trailhead.

If you're looking for something to do while here, the Horseshoe Bend Trail (see Hike 2) is just across the Mount Baker Highway, and the village of Glacier—with its general store, fine restaurants, and ski and snowboard shops—is a couple miles west.

Excelsior Group Campground: Also on the Nooksack near the site of an old turn-of-the-twentieth-century mine, this forested group campground offers two sites, each accommodating up to fifty campers. Reservations are required. The campground features pit toilets but no water; you must bring your own. Excelsior Group Campground is open from May through September. To get here, go east on the Mount Baker Highway to milepost 39.8. The campground is on the right. Nooksack Falls and the Excelsior Pass Trailhead (see Hike 12) are about a mile east of the campground.

Silver Fir Campground: Located at the bend in the road (near milepost 47) at the base of the Mount Baker Highway's final 10-mile, 3,000-foot ascent to Artist Point, this is the closest campground to the Heather Meadows Area and North Cascades National Park via Hannegan Pass. Also situated on the Nooksack River, this campground is located at the former townsite of Shuksan, which sprang up in 1898 when gold was discovered near Twin Lakes (see Hike 14) at the Lone Jack site about 5 miles northeast of here.

There are twenty forested tent and trailer sites, of which thirteen can be reserved. Along with pit toilets, running water, and three barrier-free sites, the campground offers a day-use picnic shelter. To get here, go east on the Mount Baker Highway to milepost 46.9. The campground is on the right.

Twin Lakes Road and Hannegan Pass Road, both of which lead to hiking trails with world-class views, are less than a mile from Silver Fir Campground.

Silver Lake Park: This 400-plus-acre Whatcom County park and campground is actually located about 10 miles west of the area covered in this book, but it's included because of its size and recreation opportunities. Along with eighty tent and trailer campsites (many with partial water and electricity hookups), this park features a lake for swimming and fishing, restrooms with showers and flush toilets, canoe rentals, group picnic area, horse trails and a horse camp area, and rental cabins including an eight-person overnight lodge. One wheelchair-accessible campsite is available.

To get to Silver Lake Park, head east on the Mount Baker Highway to Maple Falls (about milepost 28) and the intersection with Silver Lake Road. Turn left and continue for about 3 miles to the park, which is on your right.

To reserve a site or for information, call (360) 599-2776; e-mail SilverLake Park@co.whatcom.wa.us; or check the Whatcom County Parks and Recreation Web site at www.co.whatcom.wa.us/parks/index.jsp.

Hiker Sites

A couple trailhead hiker camps are available for those who'd like to get an early start on the trail, whether it be for mountain climbing, backpacking, or just day hiking. These are located at the trailheads for Hannegan Pass Trail (see Hike 15) and at Twin Lakes, about 7 miles up Twin Lakes Road near the trailhead for the Winchester Mountain Lookout and High Pass Trails (see Hike 14).

Backcountry Camping

Overnight camping is allowed on almost all of the trails described in the previous Day Hikes section. Set up tents in established campsites, or on rock, snow, or bare ground. Do not camp or walk on heather or other vegetation. Practice zero-impact camping. Open fires are not allowed; use camp stoves for cooking. And because all of these trails enter the Mount Baker Wilderness Area, remember that party size is limited to twelve.

Here's information on camping on individual trails.

Chain Lakes Loop Trail: Designated campsites are near Mazama and Hayes Lakes.

Lake Ann Trail: If you're entering North Cascades National Park and intend to stay overnight, a backcountry permit, available at the Glacier Public Service Center, is required.

Ptarmigan Ridge: Established campsites can be found along the Ptarmigan Ridge Trail; no camping within 1 mile of the Ptarmigan Ridge–Chain Lakes Loop junction.

Table Mountain: Because Table Mountain is very exposed, camping, while allowed, is not recommended.

Church Mountain: Set up tents on rock, snow, or bare ground. Do not camp or walk on heather or other vegetation.

Damfino Lakes–Excelsior Mountain–High Divide: There's one campsite by the lakes, some near Excelsior Pass and along High Divide. Because there's no water to be found along the ridge after snowmelt, carry your own in.

Hannegan Pass: Established campsites can be found at the trailhead; at Hannegan Camp, a signed area just off the trail about three-quarters of a mile before Hannegan Pass; and at Hannegan Peak. After the snow melts, the peak has no water, so carry your own in. About a mile beyond Hannegan Pass, the trail enters North Cascades National Park, where backcountry permits are required for overnight stays.

Heliotrope Ridge: Many climbers use this trail to access the Coleman-Deming Glacier Route to Mount Baker's summit. Camp just past the Hogs-back, located on the climbers' trail.

Skyline Divide: Find established sites along the ridge. Because there's no water to be found along the ridge after snowmelt, carry your own in.

Yellow Aster Butte: Camping is not allowed on the butte but rather at established sites in the tarn-strewn meadows below and just beyond Yellow Aster Butte.

Tomyhoi Lake: Find camping spots near the lake.

Winchester Mountain: The lookout is available for overnight camping on a first-come, first-served basis. Because there's no water to be found along the ridge after snowmelt, carry your own in.

Backpacking

A number of trails in the Mount Baker–Mount Shuksan area make for excellent backpacking adventures as well. Be sure to practice zero-impact camping, which means, among other things, pack it in and pack it out, travel and camp on durable surfaces, dispose of waste properly, leave what you find, respect wildlife, and be considerate of other visitors. Fires are not allowed in almost all of the Mount Baker Wilderness Area, which most of these trails enter. Use camp stoves for cooking. In the national park, fires are allowed at certain low-elevation camps in the Chilliwack River Valley except during burn bans. Check with the rangers at the Glacier Public Service Center for current conditions before heading out.

BP1 Copper Ridge–Chilliwack River Valley–Whatcom Pass

Because the Hannegan Pass Trail offers the easiest access to the spectacular scenery of North Cascades National Park, it's an important one for backpackers. Popular destinations are Copper Ridge, a high alpine divide with stunning views in all directions that's topped with a historic lookout tower; the Chilliwack

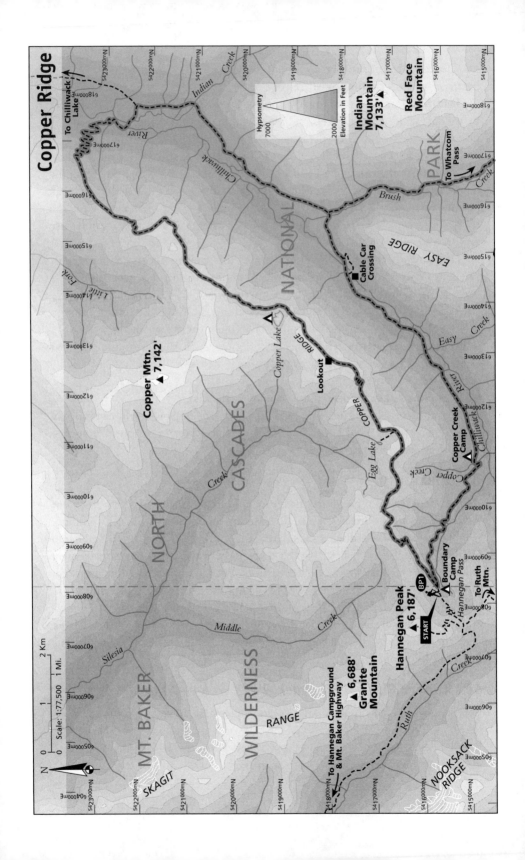

River Valley; and spectacular Whatcom Pass. The following description details a 34-mile loop with a 10-mile (round-trip) side trail that includes all three.

From Hannegan Pass (see Hike 15), continue as the trail descends for about a mile to a fork at the national park boundary. For overnight stays from here on, a backcountry permit is required and is available at the Glacier Public Service Center. (Be sure to pick one up on the way in.) Established campsites are mere yards ahead at Boundary Camp. For Copper Ridge go left at the fork and resume climbing, attaining the ridge in a little less than 2 miles from Boundary Camp. The views are grand and only become more so.

Over the next 3 miles—several tent sites to be found along the way—the trail climbs another 1,100 feet along the ridge, finally reaching the Copper Mountain Lookout, one of the few that's still a working lookout, at about 10 miles from the trailhead. Spectacular peaks, river valleys, and dense forest surround you on all sides—if mountains are your thing, here's where you want to be.

From here the trail continues along the ridge, mostly losing elevation (but occasionally climbing), for about another 5 miles. Copper Lake, about 1.5 miles past the lookout, has several tent sites. From here the trail drops at what feels like freefall speed for more than 3 miles into the Chilliwack River Valley. Heading southwest, back toward Hannegan Pass now, the trail follows the river—several tent sites to be found along the way—and intersects the Whatcom Pass Trail, 22 miles from the trailhead.

Head left for Whatcom Pass—about 5 miles and 3,000 feet of climbing away—an otherworldly place of meadows and subalpine forest at the foot of that icy tandem, Whatcom Peak and Mount Challenger. Tapto Lakes are just beyond.

Continuing our route back to Hannegan Pass, about 1.5 miles past the Whatcom Pass intersection, reach the cable car (yes, that's right) and pull yourself across the Chilliwack River. Now on the north side, follow the river for a mostly level 3 miles to Copper Creek Camp. From here it's just 2.5 miles with 1,600 feet worth of climbing back to Boundary Camp, where you went left to head toward Copper Ridge.

BP2 High Divide

With two cars, this makes a terrific, if not-too-long, point-to-point backpacking trip of up to about 11 or 12 miles: 11 if you go Damfino Lakes Trailhead to Welcome Pass Trailhead, 12 if you go Excelsior Pass Trailhead to Welcome Pass Trailhead. Look for spots to pitch your tent near Excelsior Pass and along High Divide. (See the Options section and the map under the Hike 12 trail description.) Because there's no water to be found along the ridge after snowmelt, carry your own in.

BP3 Ptarmigan Ridge–Chain Lakes Loop

Combine these two trails for a 17-mile trek, much of it above tree line, that's rich in glaciers, meadows, and alpine lakes. Start high at either the Heather Meadows Visitor Center or Artist Point. Established campsites can be found along the Ptarmigan Ridge Trail; no camping within 1 mile of the Ptarmigan Ridge–Chain Lakes Loop junction. On the Chain Lakes Loop Trail, designated campsites can be found near Mazama and Hayes Lakes. See trail descriptions and maps in Hikes 16 and 19.

Mountain Climbing and Scrambling

Mountaineering and scrambling are potentially dangerous activities, and this book does not purport to be a climbing guide as such. What follows are thumbnail sketches of some popular climbing destinations; it's up to you, the potential climber, to get proper training, including crevasse rescue techniques and glacier travel experience, as well as the proper equipment before attempting these endeavors. Also, always take into account the propensity for rapidly changing weather at high altitudes such as these. It can snow any day of the year above 5,000 feet, and visibility can quickly be reduced to nothing.

A list of climbing guide services can be found at the end of this section.

C1 Mount Baker (10,781 feet)

Each year about 5,000 people climb, or attempt to climb, to the summit of Mount Baker, and most make the approach from either the Coleman-Deming Glacier Route on the north side or the Easton Glacier Route from the south. While these routes are not technical, the ascent involves climbing 5,000 vertical feet on glacier, which implies potential dangers—crevasses, avalanches, exposure, bad weather, etc. What follows is the Coleman-Deming Glacier route. See Hike 25 in the next chapter for the Easton Glacier route.

Coleman-Deming Glacier Route: Basically, this is the route that the Edmund Coleman party used in 1868 when they made the first-ever ascent to the summit of Mount Baker. Access this route by hiking the Heliotrope Ridge Trail to the climbers' trail (see Hike 9). Reach the Hogsback at the toe of the Coleman Glacier, about 3 miles from the trailhead.

Most climbers camp here, rising at midnight or 1:00 A.M. to make the eight- to ten-hour push for the summit. It's a safer climb at night when the colder air ensures that the snow and glacier are more solid. When the sun has time to melt the snow, the likelihood of avalanches—and of melting snow bridges—increases dramatically. It's best to be on and off the glacier as early and in as little time as possible. Another popular place to camp, thus shortening the summit push, is about 1,000 feet higher on the glacier itself in a large, open, relatively crevasse-free snow bowl referred to as the Football Field.

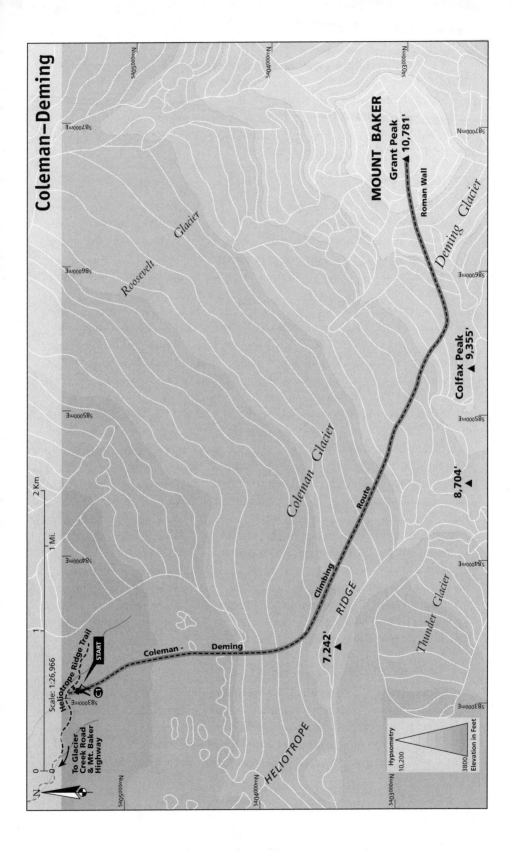

Climbers ascend the Coleman Glacier heading southeast, under the gaze of the towering Black Buttes, rock outcrops that are remnants of a bigger and much older volcano that once occupied this spot. At a saddle at about 9,000 feet, climbers reach the Deming Glacier, where they head east and climb the last 1,700-plus feet up a pumice ridge and steep (thirty-degree) snow-covered headwall.

C2 Mount Shuksan (9,131 feet)

A couple thousand people attempt the more challenging rock and glacier climb to the summit of Mount Shuksan each year. The Fisher Chimneys route is the most frequently used north-side (as in Mount Baker Highway accessed) way to the top. See Hike 31 in the next chapter for the popular and less-technical Sulphide Glacier route accessed via the south side of the Mount Baker–Mount Shuksan region.

Because Mount Shuksan requires rock climbing to scale the final 600-foot rock pyramid, it's a more technical climb than Mount Baker, and thus only a brief description is offered here. Two climbing books that describe this route in detail are published by Mountaineers Books: *Cascade Alpine Guide 3: Rainy Pass to Fraser River*, by Fred Beckey, and *Selected Climbs in the Cascades*, by Jim Nelson and Peter Potterfield.

Fisher Chimneys Route: Follow the Lake Ann Trail (see Hike 17) for about 4 miles to the saddle above the lake. Go left, following the climbers' route as it climbs east and up toward the Lower Curtis Glacier. Climbers often camp near the lake. Climbers scramble up a rocky gully through what's known as the Fisher Chimneys (named for Clarence Fisher, who led the 1927 first ascent party via this route) for a few hundred feet until they reach Winnie's Slide, a steep snow slope. Climbing east they then cross onto the Upper Curtis Glacier, where, bearing to the right (south), they make for a notch in the rock wall and an incline of crevassed snow and ice known as Hell's Highway.

Once through that, they reach the Sulphide Glacier and head north toward the obvious summit pyramid a little more than a mile away. The 600-foot summit pyramid itself offers several parallel rock gullies to the top. Most are class 3, which involves moderate exposure with frequent use of the hands; a rope should also be available.

C3 Ruth Mountain (7,115 feet)

In all those photo calendars and postcards that show the grandeur and majesty of Mount Shuksan, just out of camera range to the left is Ruth Mountain. At 7,115 feet with a small active glacier on its north side, it makes for a great first-time glacier climb or warm-up for climbing Mount Baker. In fact, from the north, where you make the approach, Mount Ruth even resembles a miniature

Fisher Chimneys

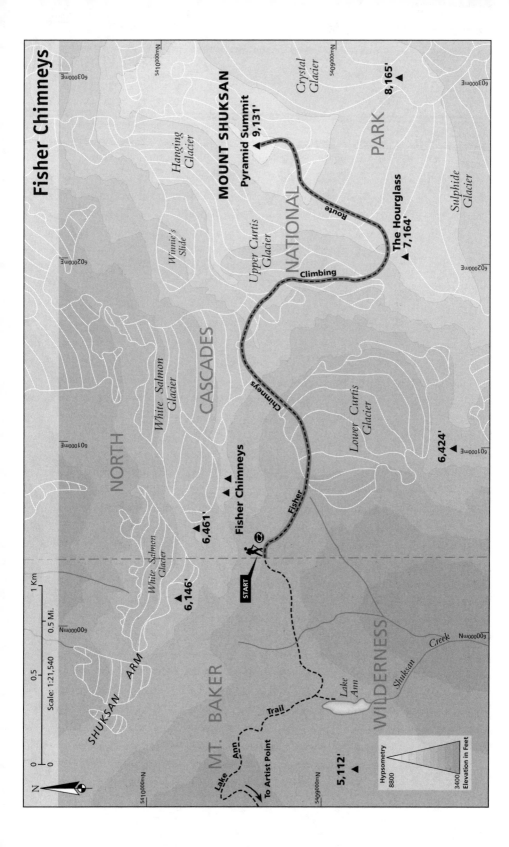

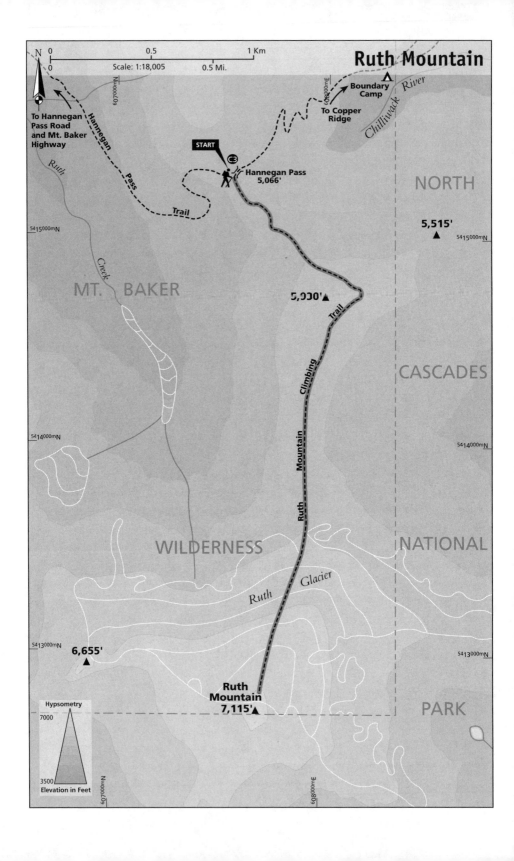

Mount Baker. And, because of its proximity to Mount Shuksan—less than 3 miles away—the alpine views are spectacular, especially those of Shuksan's rarely seen north side including the Nooksack Cirque, the source of the Nooksack River's North Fork.

I have a friend who describes Ruth Mountain as "the best cheeseburger you've ever had in your life"—just a totally enjoyable experience. Not a strenuous two-day, one-night slog like climbing Mount Baker or Mount Shuksan but rather a nice one-day, challenging enough, views-maybe-even-better-than-Baker-or-Shuksan climb that has you back in your own bed that night. Though not a particularly technical climb, the route does ascend about 1,000 feet of the Ruth Glacier, which means climbers should take appropriate glacier travel precautions (rope up, etc.) and carry proper equipment (ice axes, pickets and flukes, etc.).

To get to Ruth Mountain, follow the Hannegan Pass Trail (see Hike 15) to the pass. Once there look for a climbers' trail that heads south and down into a meadowy area. Soon enough it does what climbers' trails tend to do: get to the top of something as quickly as it can. In this case the trail climbs seemingly straight up a heathery slope. Once at the top it contours to the left (east) and then south, gradually climbing on an exposed talus slope (or snow slope, early in the season) around a rocky knob.

Heading south now, Ruth Mountain directly ahead, follow the ridge to the foot of Ruth Glacier about three-quarters of a mile ahead. From here it's about 1,000 feet via a twenty- to twenty-five-degree snow slope to the summit. Ruth Mountain is also popular with backcountry skiers and snowboarders.

Scrambles

These are climbs—often over snow or rock—that lead to a summit but don't require the use of a rope or other technical equipment. In this book they're basically peaks you can get to by hiking or climbing beyond where the maintained trail ends. These are fun if you've got a bit of the peak-bagger mentality but not all the equipment, time, or training to go for bigger summits.

Though they're generally class 2 (involving the use of hands but not a rope) and class 3 (involving moderate exposure with frequent use of hands; a rope should be available), the potential for danger exists. Be careful and don't climb beyond your abilities and comfort level. (Again, this is not a climbing guide, so the scrambles included are pretty straightforward.)

Tomyhoi Peak (7,451 feet): Follow the Yellow Aster Butte Trail (see Hike 13) to the trail intersection just before the last push to the top of the butte. Go left and drop down into Yellow Aster Meadows. Tomyhoi Peak, all 7,451 feet of it, is the prominent peak in the near distance to the north, notable for its craggy summit horn and shelflike plateau on its east flank. Bear to the right (north) through the peaceful lake- and mining-equipment-strewn area, following the boot trail as it eventually starts climbing steeply up heathered slopes.

For the most part, the trail is easy to follow as it roller-coasters up and down several rocky ridges. It's when it gets to talus slopes on the peak's east slope that the trail becomes hard to follow. Look for cairns (piles of stones). You'll soon find yourself on the north side of the mountain at the top of a glacier. Using your ice ax, traverse the top of the glacier for about 50 yards and return to the rock, where the scrambling begins. Handholds are plentiful, and trending northwest, climb as high and as far as your comfort level allows. You'll reach a false summit, then drop about 100 feet to a notch only to regain that 100 feet almost immediately. Staying to the left of the ridge, continue climbing for a few hundred feet to the summit. Some parts of this last section feel a bit exposed; you may want to use a rope or just find a nice flat spot and call it a summit. Why not? You're close enough.

Distance from Yellow Aster Butte Trail junction: 3.5 miles (one way); total distance from Yellow Aster Butte Trailhead: 7 miles, for a 14-mile round-trip.

Yellow Aster Butte (6,241 feet): Follow the Yellow Aster Butte Trail (see Hike 13) all the way to the end at the top of the butte. But wait, there's more. Once at the top, follow the climbers' trail north for about a quarter mile to a summit that's just a skosh higher—6,241 feet versus 6,100 feet.

Hannegan Peak (6,187 feet): While certainly strenuous because of its steep grade, this is one of the least technical peaks you'll ever bag. And my, oh my, the grand Cascade views from the summit are just about as good as they get in the North Cascades. From Hannegan Pass (see Hike 15) follow the steep trail north, climbing 1,100 feet in 1.2 miles to the obvious summit. Consider spending the night at the top; a cluster of hearty trees provides just enough shield from the wind.

Coleman Pinnacle (6,403 feet): This prominent shark-fin-like rock is accessed from the Ptarmigan Ridge Trail (see Hike 19), about 3 miles from the intersection with the Chain Lakes Loop Trail. Its proximity to Mount Baker's summit, just 4.5 miles away, makes for spectacular full-face Baker views. Be aware that snow lingers long into summer here. Do not climb beyond your abilities.

With Coleman Pinnacle in sight ahead of you, follow the trail for about 3 miles, actually passing just beyond and below the pinnacle. Ascend toward an obvious saddle at the peak's shoulder and proceed right (east) toward the pinnacle. Reach the top after about a 150-foot scramble.

Mountain Guides

The following guide services offer mountain- and rock-climbing instruction, guiding, or both in the Mount Baker–Mount Shuksan area.

- Alpine Ascents International, (206) 378–1927, www.alpineascents.com
- American Alpine Institute, (360) 671–1505, www.mtnguide.com

- Base Camp, Inc., (360) 733–5461, www.basecampwa.com
- Mountain Madness, (206) 937–8389, www.mountainmadness.com

River Rafting

From June through August a 9-mile stretch of the North Fork Nooksack River between Glacier and Maple Falls offers a heck of a roller-coaster ride for adventurous river rafters. The rapids are mostly class 3 and 4 with the scariest section (or most exciting, depending on your view) being the first mile after the put-in at the Horseshoe Bend Trailhead. Farther downstream, the river eventually mellows to the point where the last 6 miles can be a tame river float.

While white-water rafting is great fun, in the glacier-fed, boulder- and snag-riddled Nooksack, it can be quite dangerous, especially the first 3 miles. Every few years, it seems, the local newspaper runs a series of stories about safe river rafting, inevitably after someone has drowned in a rafting incident.

For that reason it's best to go with one of the several rafting companies that are permitted by the Forest Service to run guided trips. They provide rafts, transportation to the river, and safety equipment.

River Guides

The following guide services offer white-water rafting trips on a 9-mile stretch of the Nooksack River between Glacier and Maple Falls.

- Alpine Adventures, (800) 723–8386, www.alpineadventures.com
- River Recreation, (800) 464–5899, www.riverrecreation.com
- River Riders, (800) 448–7238, www.riverrider.com

Biking

Mountain Biking

The Mount Baker–Mount Shuksan area is certainly a destination spot for hikers and climbers, but in truth, it's a bit less so for those of the knobby-tire persuasion. On all but one of the national forest or national park trails that fall within the area covered in this book, bikes are prohibited. (That trail is the Canyon Ridge Trail, described later in this section.)

However, Forest Service roads are open to mountain bikers, and many of these roads offer great views and big climbs with fast descents, if not a whit of challenging singletrack riding. (Challenging in terms of climbing, yes, but not in terms of maneuvering around and through obstacles—see Road Biking section for that.) The following are some of the more ridden Forest Service roads. All are gravel unless otherwise noted.

Cyclist approaches the Mount Baker Hill Climb finish line

Forest Service Road 37: Also known as Deadhorse Creek Road, this road follows the North Fork of the Nooksack River for several miles of gravel road before heading south and up—very up. Eventually, it leads almost 13 miles—climbing 3,400 feet along the way—to the Skyline Divide Trail. Access this road at the Mount Baker Highway milepost 34.3. Turn right onto Glacier Creek Road (Forest Service Road 39) and almost immediately left onto FR 37.

Forest Service Road 32 (Hannegan Pass Road): This road also follows the Nooksack River, albeit a bit closer to its source, and from time to time offers awesome views of Mount Shuksan. Not too steep, it climbs about 1,100 feet over 5.3 miles to the Hannegan Pass Trailhead at road's end. Go east on the Mount Baker Highway to about a half mile past milepost 46. Hannegan Pass Road is on your left.

Forest Service Road 3070 (Razor Hone Road): Located across the river from Hannegan Pass Road, Razor Hone Road follows the river east for about 3 miles. Go east on the Mount Baker Highway to about three-quarters of a mile past milepost 46. Razor Hone Road is on your left.

Forest Service Road 31 (Canyon Creek Road): This mixed paved and gravel road leads about 15 miles around and to the north side of Church Mountain, climbing fairly consistently much of the way. Numerous offshoot roads lead off from Canyon Creek Road, which, if they're not gated, are fair game for riding.

To get to Canyon Creek Road, go east on the Mount Baker Highway to milepost 35.4 and signed Canyon Creek Road (FR 31) on your left.

Canyon Ridge Trail: This is the one national forest trail in the area that's open to bikes, and in truth, it's probably not worth the effort. Along with being extremely primitive, this 10-mile-long (one way) trail is usually snow-covered, rarely maintained, and often overgrown; riders end up spending much of their time carrying their bikes over unridable sections. That said, here's how to get there.

Follow Canyon Creek Road (Forest Service Road 31, described earlier) to the end. Follow the Damfino Lakes Trail for about three-quarters of a mile to a signed junction. Go left following the sign for Canyon Ridge Trail and Boundary Way Trail. In another half mile, go left at another junction; you're now on the Canyon Ridge Trail.

Now, if you're the type of mountain biker who's into free riding—that is, flying downhill, jumping off stumps and rocks, and catching big-time air, a scene is emerging near the town of Glacier. A local logging company is allowing trails to be built on mountainous land just south of town. For more information, stop by the Glacier Ski Shop (9966 Mount Baker Highway in Glacier; 360–599–1943), which rents specially equipped bikes and in summer offers guided rides.

Road Biking

Because the shoulders on winding Mount Baker Highway are not especially wide, road biking can be somewhat dangerous. Still, many hardy cyclists use the road for epic training rides, especially the last 10 miles to Artist Point, which climb about 3,000 feet. There's even a race—the Mount Baker Hill Climb—held in early September from Glacier to Artist Point. The 24.5-mile race climbs 4,300 feet.

South Side

Driving Tour

Baker Lake Road (also known as Forest Service Road 11 on the north end where it enters the Mount Baker–Snoqualmie National Forest) leads north for 26 miles from Highway 20, about 15 miles east of Sedro-Woolley. The first 20 miles are paved; the last 6 are gravel and in summer tend to be dusty. What follows are access points, listed by milepost number, of various viewpoints, campgrounds, access roads, and other points of interest.

Because this road tops out at only about 1,150 feet, it is not always snow-covered throughout the winter. Check the Web site at www.fs.fed.us/r6/mbs or call the ranger (360–856–5700) for the latest conditions.

MP 0.3, Creekside Camping and Grocery: Private campground with store.

MP 4.8, Grandy Lake Park: This Skagit County Park offers camping, picnicking, fishing, and boating on a small lake about 8 miles south of Baker Lake.

MP 6.6, Burpee Hill Road: Leads south for 4 miles to downtown Concrete.

MP 7.3: After rounding a bend, you're struck by the first south-side views of Mount Shuksan, a frosty white massif topped by a rocky, sky-reaching pyramid. The broad white expanse is the Sulphide Glacier, which, as the most popular route for climbers, is often crawling with the cramponed and carabinered set.

MP 11.9: Enter the Mount Baker–Snoqualmie National Forest. (From here on out, a Northwest Forest Pass is required to park at any trailhead.)

MP 12.2, Forest Service Road 12: This gravel road leads to the Mount Baker National Recreation Area, an 8,600-acre year-round forest and alpine wonderland crisscrossed with miles of hiking, equestrian, cross-country skiing, mountaineering, and snowshoe trails and routes. You'll find relatively easy access to everything from dense forests to alpine meadows, glacial moraines, cascading creeks and waterfalls, panoramic mountain vistas, and much more.

Forest Service Road 12 leads to Forest Service Road 13, which ends at Schreibers Meadow, a popular starting point for many mountain activities. Popular trails such as Scott Paul, Railroad Grade, Dock Butte, and Park Butte Lookout are accessed via the FR 12 turnoff from Baker Lake Road.

MP 13.6: Catch the first views of Mount Baker. From this southeast aspect, much of the Sherman Crater is hidden, and the 10,781-foot volcano appears more symmetrical than from other angles, almost Fujilike.

MP 13.7, Baker Lake Dam Road (Forest Service Road 1106): This gravel road leads 1.3 miles to Kulshan Campground (see Camping section later in this chapter) and a nice vista overlooking the lake and both Mounts Baker and

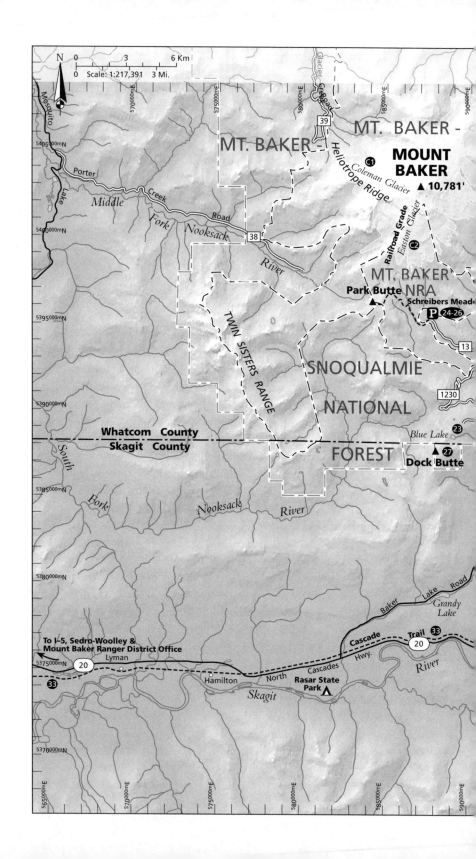

N 0   3   6 Km

Scale: 1:217,391 3 Mi.

Mosquito

MT. BAKER -

MT. BAKER -

MOUNT
BAKER
▲ 10,781'

Coleman Glacier C1

Glacier Creek

39

Heliotrope Ridge

Lake

Porter   Creek

Middle   Fork   Road

Nooksack

38

River

5405000mN

5400000mN

5395000mN

5390000mN

Railroad Grade   Easton Glacier C2

MT. BAKER
NRA

Park Butte ▲

Schreibers Mead

P 24-26

13

1230

TWIN SISTERS RANGE

SNOQUALMIE

NATIONAL

Blue Lake 23

Whatcom County
Skagit County

South

FOREST ▲ 27
Dock Butte

Fork

Nooksack   River

5385000mN

5380000mN

Baker   Lake   Road

Grandy
Lake

To I–5, Sedro-Woolley &
Mount Baker Ranger District Office

Cascade   Trail 33

20

Lyman

Cascades   Hwy.   20   River

33

Hamilton   North   Rasar State
Park ▲

Cascades

Skagit

5375000mN

5370000mN

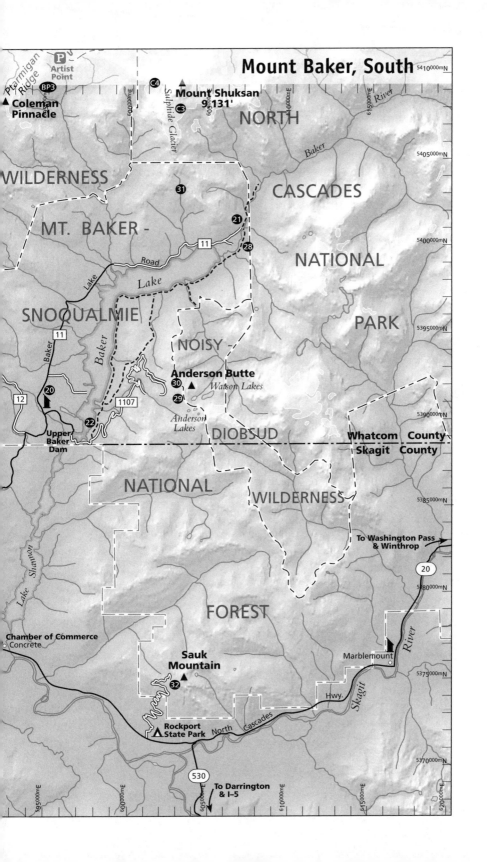

Ptarmigan Ridge

P Artist Point

BP3

▲ Coleman Pinnacle

C4

▲ Mount Shuksan 9,131'

C3

Sulphide Glacier

NORTH

Baker River

5410000mN

600000mE

605000mE

615000mE

5405000mN

WILDERNESS

31

21

CASCADES

5400000mN

MT. BAKER -

11

28

Road

Lake

NATIONAL

5395000mN

Lake

SNOQUALMIE

11

Baker

NOISY -

PARK

20

12

1107

Anderson Butte

30 ▲ Watson Lakes

29

Anderson Lakes

5390000mN

22

Upper Baker Dam

DIOBSUD

Whatcom County

Skagit County

5385000mN

NATIONAL

WILDERNESS

Lake Shannon

To Washington Pass & Winthrop

20

5380000mN

FOREST

Chamber of Commerce
○ Concrete

Sauk Mountain

32 ▲

Marblemount

Skagit River

5375000mN

Hwy.

Rockport State Park

North Cascades

5370000mN

530

To Darrington & I-5

595000mE

600000mE

605000mE

610000mE

615000mE

620000mE

Shuksan. Puget Sound Energy's Baker Lake Lodge, a conference center available for public rental, is located here also. Call (888) 711–3033 for information.

About 1.8 miles from Baker Lake Road, the road (now paved) narrows to one lane and crosses the top of Baker Lake Dam. Once across, the road becomes Forest Service Road 1107, which offers access to the lakeside Baker Lake Trail and the Anderson-Watson Lakes area, a popular hiking, fishing, and backcountry camping destination (see Hike 29).

MP 14.5, Shadow of the Sentinels Trail: Here you can enjoy a peaceful, paved half-mile traipse through old-growth, moss-hung forest complete with interpretive signage (see Hike 20).

MP 15.2, Horseshoe Cove Campground: Turn right down Forest Service Road 1168 and follow it for about 2 miles to this lakeside campground (see Camping section later in this chapter). Picnic tables provide day-use opportunities.

MP 17.9, Boulder Creek Campground: This campground is located on Boulder Creek, fed by Mount Baker's Boulder Glacier. (See the Camping section later in this chapter.)

MP 18.1, Forest Service Road 1130: This often-unsigned gravel road offers access to the Boulder Ridge Trail, an access route for those climbing Mount Baker via the Boulder Glacier Route.

MP 19.3, Panorama Point Campground: As its name suggests, this campground offers expansive lake and mountain views. Picnic tables provide day-use opportunities.

MP 20.0, Baker Lake Resort: Here you'll find a campground, cabin rental, boat launch, and the only store for miles around. Open from May through September. (See Camping section later in this chapter.)

MP 20.0, Park Creek Campground: This spot offers secluded creekside campsites in the woods. (See Camping section later in this chapter.)

MP 20.4: Pavement ends. The remaining 5.6 miles of road are gravel and can be dusty in summer.

MP 21.1: The first views of Baker Lake (from the road) occur here. Partially obstructed views continue for the next 5 miles to the end of the road.

MP 23.5, Shannon Creek Campground: This campground also has picnic tables for day-use opportunities.

MP 23.5, Forest Service Road 1152: This gravel road offers access to the Shannon Ridge Trail, a popular hiking spot and access route for climbers heading to the summit of Mount Shuksan (see Hike 31).

MP 26: This is the end of the road and the trailhead for the Baker River and Baker Lake (North Entrance) Trails (see Hikes 21 and 28). Here you'll find a few primitive campsites and a nice place to access the Baker River.

A massive fir along the Shadow of the Sentinels Trail

Easy Hikes and Walks

Unless indicated otherwise, a Northwest Forest Pass is required to park at trail-heads for all of the following hikes and walks. Unless noted, dogs are allowed as long as they're leashed. With the exception of the Blue Lake Trail, the following easy walks and hikes are at a low enough elevation that they're often passable year-round. For the most up-to-date information on conditions, call the Mount Baker Ranger District in Sedro-Woolley at (360) 856–5700.

20 Shadow of the Sentinels Trail

TYPE OF TRAIL: Barrier-free; hikers and walkers only; interpretive signs.

TOTAL DISTANCE: 0.5-mile loop.

TIME REQUIRED: 30 minutes.

DIFFICULTY LEVEL: Easy.

ELEVATION GAIN: 30 feet.

MAPS: Green Trails Lake Shannon 46.

STARTING POINT: Go east on Highway 20 to just past milepost 82, about 15 miles past Sedro-Woolley. Turn left onto Baker Lake Road. Continue for about 15 miles. The trailhead parking lot is on the right.

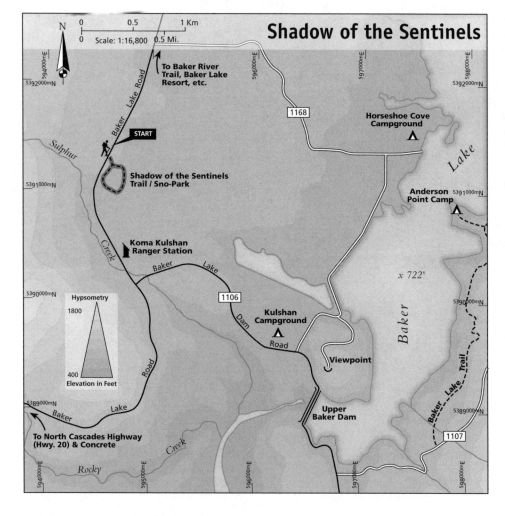

THE HIKE: Once out of the car, take note of the huge, 500-year-old slice of Douglas fir in the first of several interpretive displays. (If you've got about a half hour, try to count all the rings.) It's a hint of what you'll see on the trail, but thankfully, those are still standing.

Starting out as boardwalk, the trail, which soon turns to pavement, winds through otherworldly old-growth forest, including some of the oldest trees in the area. It's all ferns and nurse logs and moss- and lichen-hung cedars, firs, and hemlocks. Chances are it'll remind you of something out of the *Lord of the Rings* movies. Signs point out the biggie—a Douglas fir 7 feet in diameter—but its sheer size would point it out anyway.

This is a short walk, so take your time: read the signs and learn about old-growth forest, an unfortunately all too rapidly vanishing wonder. One sign quotes Robert Frost, and then adds its own worthwhile sentiment:

> "The woods are lovely, dark and deep,"
> and all of us, as stewards of this forest,
> have promises to keep.

21 Baker River Trail

See map on pages 96–97.

TYPE OF TRAIL: Hiking only.

TOTAL DISTANCE: 5.2 miles out-and-back.

TIME REQUIRED: 3 hours.

DIFFICULTY LEVEL: Easy.

ELEVATION GAIN: 400 feet.

MAPS: Green Trails Lake Shannon 46, Mount Shuksan 14.

STARTING POINT: Go east on Highway 20 to just past milepost 82, about 15 miles past Sedro-Woolley. Turn left onto Baker Lake Road. Continue for 26 miles to the road-end trailhead parking lot.

THE HIKE: Get set for stately, moss-hung old-growth forest (including cedars that somehow seem to grow right out of boulders), ponds built by industrious beavers who forever seem to be changing the course of the river, and a number of rushing, glacier-fed creeks. And luckily, because this trail is at a relatively low elevation, it's hikable almost year-round.

The trail parallels the river and for the first half mile or so is barrier-free, allowing small children or those with disabilities the opportunity to experience the river environment. At about the half-mile mark, go straight at the intersection with the Baker Lake Trail, which crosses the river to the right.

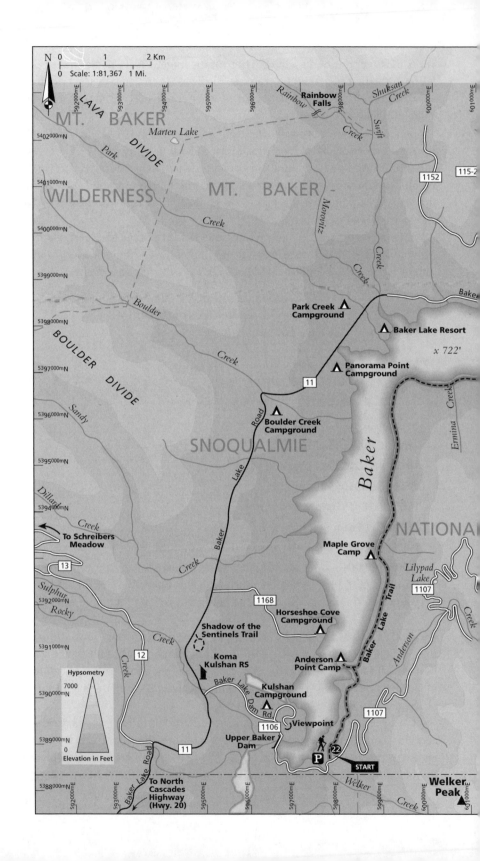

N 0   1   2 Km
0   Scale: 1:81,367   1 Mi.

MT. BAKER

LAVA   DIVIDE

Rainbow   Rainbow Falls

Shuksan Creek

Swift Creek

WILDERNESS

MT.   BAKER -

Marten Lake

5402000mN

5401000mN

5400000mN

Park Creek

Morovitz Creek

Creek

1152

115-2

5399000mN

Boulder

Baker

5398000mN

Park Creek Campground

Baker Lake Resort

x 722'

BOULDER DIVIDE

Creek

5397000mN

Panorama Point Campground

11

5396000mN

Sandy

Boulder Creek Campground

SNOQUALMIE

5395000mN

Baker

5394000mN

Dillard

Creek

To Schreibers Meadow

Maple Grove Camp

NATIONAL

Lilypad Lake

13

1107

Sulphur

5392000mN

Rocky

1168

Horseshoe Cove Campground

Baker Lake Trail

Creek

Shadow of the Sentinels Trail

Anderson

5391000mN

12

Koma Kulshan RS

Anderson Point Camp

Creek

Hypsometry

7000

5390000mN

Baker Lake Dam

Kulshan Campground

1107

Elevation in Feet

0

5389000mN

Rd.

1106

Viewpoint

Upper Baker Dam

1107

Baker Lake Road

11

22

P

START

5388000mN

To North Cascades Highway (Hwy. 20)

Welker

Welker Peak

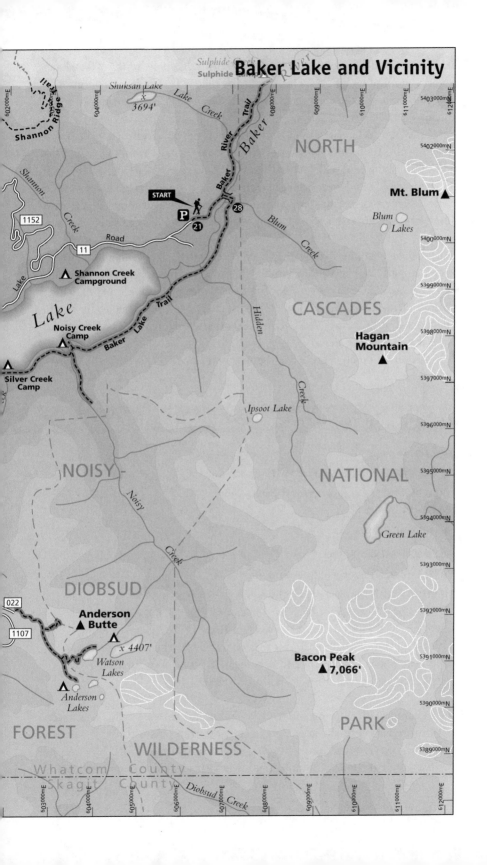

Sulphide Creek
Sulphide

Shuksan Lake
x
3694'

Ilett Ridge
Shannon Ridge

Lake Creek

River Trail

Baker River

NORTH

Mt. Blum ▲

Blum Lakes

START
P
21
28

Baker

Shannon Creek

1152

Road
11

Shannon Creek
Campground

Lake

Blum Creek

CASCADES

Baker Lake Trail

Noisy Creek
Camp

Silver Creek
Camp

Hidden

Creek

Hagan
Mountain
▲

Ipsoot Lake

NOISY-

Noisy

NATIONAL

Green Lake

Creek

DIOBSUD

022

1107

Anderson
▲ Butte

x 4407'

Watson
Lakes

Anderson
Lakes

Bacon Peak
▲ 7,066'

FOREST

WILDERNESS

PARK

Whatcom County
Skagit County

Diobsud Creek

(*Note:* Heavy floods in October 2003 caused serious damage to the Baker Lake Trail and several of its bridges; check with the ranger for the latest conditions.) Almost immediately, the trail narrows and takes a turn for the slightly more technical.

Over the next mile, the trail meanders away from the river for a stretch and climbs a bit into the forest. When next you see the river, it's rushing and gushing with minirapids and whirlpools all aswirl. That doesn't last. Again the trail leaves the riverside and after crossing a creek over a wood bridge enters a land of silent ancient forest. You soon come upon ponds—beaver ponds abuzz with wildlife—and the water here is usually as calm and placid as the river was raging earlier.

Ahead, just past the 2-mile mark, enter North Cascades National Park. (Dogs are not allowed beyond this point.) About a half mile ahead, the trail ends at Sulphide Creek, a rushing tumbler from the flanks of Mount Shuksan, which you can see from the water's edge. Pull up a creekside rock, have some lunch, and be wowed at how water and gravity eventually turn massive boulders into the smallest of cobblestones.

Reverse direction and return via the way you came.

22 Baker Lake Trail–South Entrance

See map on pages 96–97.

TYPE OF TRAIL: Hiking and equestrian use only.

TOTAL DISTANCE: 4 miles out-and-back.

TIME REQUIRED: 3 hours.

DIFFICULTY LEVEL: Easy.

ELEVATION GAIN: 300 feet.

MAPS: Green Trails Lake Shannon 46.

STARTING POINT: Go east on Highway 20 to just past milepost 82, about 15 miles past Sedro-Woolley. Turn left onto Baker Lake Road and follow it for 13.8 miles to Baker Lake Dam Road (Forest Service Road 1106). Continue for about 3 miles—along the way, the road crosses the top of the Baker Lake Dam and becomes Forest Service Road 1107— to the trailhead parking lot, which is on the left.

THE HIKE: Along with offering superb lake and mountain views, this trail offers a brief history lesson of the area. At the start the trail passes through a stately forest of majestic Douglas firs that got their start in life in 1843. How do we know that's their birthday? Because that's the year a small eruption on Mount

Tree stumps line much of the bottom of Baker Lake

Baker wiped out their predecessors. Amazingly, cedar snags from the former forest are still standing.

Sidehilling above Baker Lake, the trail offers occasional lake and mountain views as it passes in and out of little ravines. At about 1.7 miles, the trail crosses rushing Anderson Creek over a bridge. Just ahead, go left on the spur trail, which leads down to Anderson Point, a spit jutting into the lake. This point makes a terrific lunch and turnaround spot. Views are grand and, when the lake level is low, include the somewhat eerie stumps that line the lake bed, evidence of the forest that was here before the lake basin was flooded in 1959 for construction of the Baker Lake Dam.

To return, take the same route back. *Note:* The main trail, which continues north for another 12 miles, was a nineteenth-century lumbering and mining route.

23 Blue Lake Trail

TYPE OF TRAIL: Hiking only.

TOTAL DISTANCE: 1.4 miles out-and-back.

TIME REQUIRED: 2 hours.

DIFFICULTY LEVEL: Easy.

ELEVATION GAIN: 300 feet.

MAPS: Green Trails Hamilton 45.

STARTING POINT: Go east on Highway 20 to just past milepost 82. Turn left onto Baker Lake Road and in 12.2 miles, turn left onto Forest Service Road 12. Follow it for 6.8 miles (continuing straight at the intersection with Forest Service Road 13 at 3 miles) and turn left onto

Mirror reflection in Blue Lake

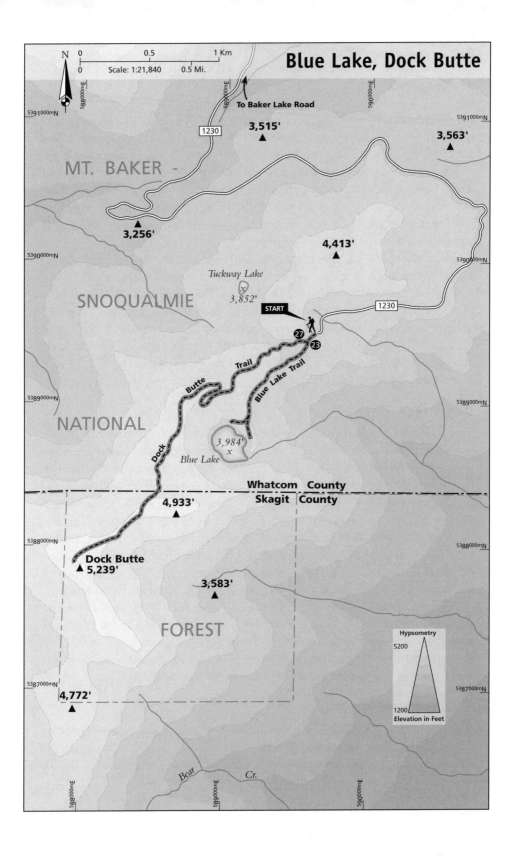

Blue Lake, Dock Butte

N

Scale: 1:21,840

0 0.5 1 Km
0   0.5 Mi.

To Baker Lake Road

1230

3,515' ▲

3,563' ▲

MT. BAKER -

3,256' ▲

4,413' ▲

SNOQUALMIE

Tuckway Lake
x
3,852'

START

1230

27
23

Butte   Trail

Blue Lake Trail

Dock

3,984'
x

Blue Lake

NATIONAL

Whatcom   County
Skagit   County

4,933' ▲

Dock Butte
▲ **5,239'**

3,583' ▲

FOREST

4,772'
▲

Hypsometry

5200

1200
Elevation in Feet

Forest Service Road 1230. Follow it for 3.8 miles to the road-end trail-head.

THE HIKE: A peaceful mountain lake surrounded by high rock walls, alpine meadows, and heavy timber rewards hikers on this short jaunt. The trail itself offers some ups and downs but is short enough (0.7 mile each way) that kids will get a kick out of it. Once at the lake, a number of exploratory trails lead off to the left to better and better views. Follow the sound of gushing water and you'll no doubt spot the string of small waterfalls, plunging and tumbling over one another. Given the trail's brevity, and big-time payoff, don't be surprised if you're not alone.

From the trailhead, hike through an old clear-cut into heavy forest, being sure to follow the newer, obvious rerouted trail. At about a quarter mile, go left at the signed intersection with the Dock Butte Trail (see Hike 27). *(Note:* Since the Dock Butte Trail hike is only about 1.5 miles each way, consider adding that to your excursion. Be aware, however, that that trail climbs about 1,300 feet.)

Reach the lake after about a half mile more of gentle ups and downs, some of which can be muddy. At a fork just above the lake, choose the left. There's more room for exploration that way.

Day Hikes

The following are longer trails, most of which are 4 to 10 miles in length (round-trip) and require 1,000 or more feet of elevation gain. These trails are well marked and easy to follow. However, they can be subject to harsh weather conditions. Blowdown and washout are common and can make trails impassable. For the most up-to-date information on conditions, call the Mount Baker Ranger District in Sedro-Woolley at (360) 856–5700. The Mount Baker–Snoqualmie National Forest Web site (www.fs.fed.us/r6/mbs) is also a good source for trail conditions, though it's still best to call. From July through October most of the following trails are snow-free enough for hiking, but before heading out, it's always good to check with the ranger for the latest conditions.

Unless indicated otherwise, a Northwest Forest Pass is required to park at the following trailheads. Cost is $5.00 for a daily pass or $30.00 for an annual pass. Passes are available at the Glacier Public Service Center, the Mount Baker Ranger District office in Sedro-Woolley, and numerous outlets in the area. Finally, unless noted, dogs are allowed as long as they're leashed.

Schreibers Meadow

Schreibers Meadow is kind of like a Heather Meadows on the south side of Mount Baker, albeit with more of a wilderness feel—no pavement, no buses, pit toilets, no picnic tables (though there is a hitching post for stock animals). It's

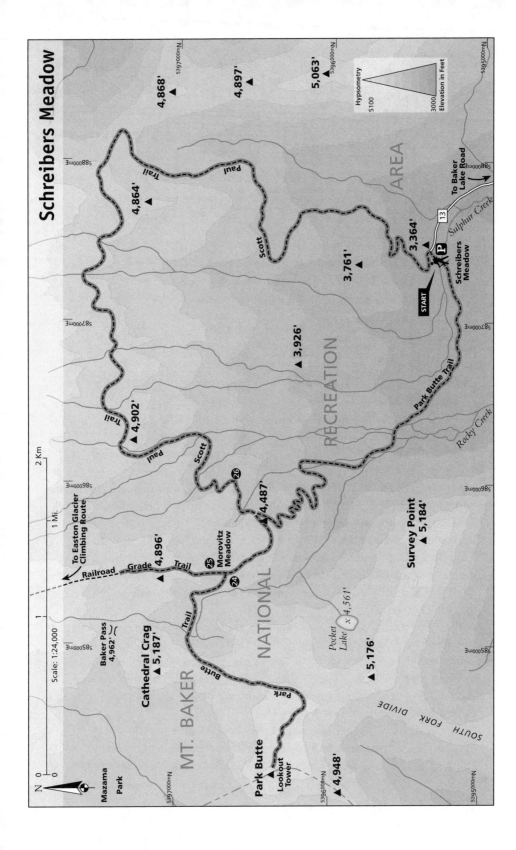

Schreibers Meadow

N

Scale: 1:24,000

0   1   2 Km
0   1 Mi.

Hypsometry

5100   3000

Elevation in Feet

MT. BAKER

NATIONAL

RECREATION

AREA

Mazama Park

To Easton Glacier Climbing Route

Baker Pass
4,962'

Railroad   Grade   Trail

Cathedral Crag
▲ 5,187'

4,896' ▲

Paul

Scott

Trail

26

Morovitz Meadow

25

24

▲ 4,487'

Park   Butte   Trail

Park Butte
Lookout Tower

▲ 4,948'

Pocket
Lake   x 4,561'

▲ 5,176'

Survey Point
▲ 5,184'

SOUTH FORK DIVIDE

Rocky Creek

Park Butte Trail

START

P

Schreibers Meadow

13

To Baker
Lake Road

Sulphur Creek

3,364'

3,761'

▲ 3,926'

Scott

Paul   Trail

4,864' ▲

4,868' ▲

4,897' ▲

5,063'

4,902' ▲

Paul   Trail

just a jumping-off point for several terrific hikes, mountaineering routes, camping areas, and, in early fall, blueberry picking. Also a draw: glorious meadows of heather and wildflowers.

Schreibers Meadow is the site of a lava flow that took place about 10,000 years ago from a parasitic minivolcano. That's the closest the present Mount Baker has come to erupting. So far.

24 Park Butte Trail

See map on page 103.

TYPE OF TRAIL: Hiking; equestrian use from August 1 through October 31.

TOTAL DISTANCE: 7 miles out-and-back.

TIME REQUIRED: 4 hours.

DIFFICULTY LEVEL: Difficult.

ELEVATION GAIN: 2,100 feet.

MAPS: Green Trails Hamilton 45.

STARTING POINT: Go east on Highway 20 to just past milepost 82. Turn left onto Baker Lake Road and in about 12.2 miles, turn left onto Forest Service Road 12. In 3 miles, turn right onto Forest Service Road 13 and follow it for 6 miles to the road-end parking lot.

THE HIKE: Built in 1933 and used for fire surveillance until the early 1960s, the Park Butte Lookout is not only maintained and open to the public but also available for camping on a first-come, first-served basis. With the icy south flank of Mount Baker just 2 air miles away to the north and the rust-colored Twin Sisters Range just 4 miles to the west, this truly is a room with a view, as well as just a neat hiking destination. (Interestingly, in the mid-1970s when there was fear of a Mount Baker eruption, the lookout became an observatory for volcano monitors.)

From the trailhead map kiosk, follow the obvious trail to the right. In about a hundred yards, just after the Scott Paul Trail (see Hike 26) sign, cross the Sulphur Creek bridge. Pass through Schreibers Meadow, a short but lush stretch bursting with heathers, huckleberries, wildflowers, and seemingly countless exploratory trails leading to just as many tiny ponds and wetlands. Views of Mount Baker emerge through the trees.

Back on the main trail, the way climbs steeply and ruggedly and in about a mile reaches ever-meandering and aptly named Rocky Creek. (*Note:* Floods in fall 2003 destroyed a bridge here and moved the creek about 100 yards west;

Hiker descending after a visit to Park Butte Lookout

check with the ranger at 360–856–5700 for the latest conditions.) Chances are, you'll be rock-hopping for a bit and crossing over a log or two. Most likely you'll end up with wet feet.

Once you're across, the trail resumes climbing steeply and at about 2 miles reaches another junction with the Scott Paul Trail. (This is the other end of the Scott Paul Trail loop.) Just ahead reach Morovitz Meadow, a sublime area with grand mountain and meadow views. It's named after "Mighty Joe" Morovitz, a mountain man if there ever was one, and a homesteader who called this south side of Mount Baker home in the late 1800s and early 1900s. He mined, prospected, farmed, guided mountaineering expeditions in the area— you name it—and it wasn't unusual for him to haul 100 pounds of supplies on his back for the 32-mile trip from the Skagit River pioneer town of Birdsview to his mountain home.

Continue climbing, going straight at the signed intersection with the Railroad Grade Trail, and after crossing a creek and passing through more meadows, follow the trail as it swings south and begins a steep rocky climb toward the lookout. Continue left at the signed intersection with the Mazama Park and the Bell Pass Trails. Look up and to the right; you can see the building. You'll see Pocket Lake to the south and, when the trail swings back again to the north, the stunning Twin Sisters Range. It's composed of dunite (mostly olivine for you rock hounds keeping score at home), thus its reddish-orange hue. The range is actually from the earth's mantle, emerging from about 10 miles deep inside the earth.

At about 3.5 miles from the trailhead, reach the lookout and thank the Skagit Alpine Club, which maintains the lookout, for keeping it in such great shape. Wow at the views, which are among the best you'll find in the North Cascades. That massive, white slab of ice creeping up the side of Mount Baker is the Easton Glacier; Railroad Grade is the lateral moraine heading up the mountain in an even, almost straight line. Look for hikers and mountaineers making their way for the summit up one of the most popular mountaineering routes.

The craggy peaks just to the west (left) of Mount Baker are the Black Buttes. They're remnants of a much bigger volcano that once occupied pretty much the same spot as the present Mount Baker.

25 Railroad Grade Trail

See map on page 103.

TYPE OF TRAIL: Hiking only.

TOTAL DISTANCE: 6 miles, out-and-back.

TIME REQUIRED: 4 hours.

DIFFICULTY LEVEL: Difficult.

ELEVATION GAIN: 1,600 feet.

MAPS: Green Trails Hamilton 45.

STARTING POINT: Go east on Highway 20 to just past milepost 82. Turn left onto Baker Lake Road and in about 12.2 miles, turn left onto Forest Service Road 12. In 3 miles, turn right onto Forest Service Road 13 and follow it for 6 miles to the road-end parking lot.

THE HIKE: Follow the Park Butte Trail description (see Hike 24) for about 2-plus miles to the intersection with the Railroad Grade Trail in Morovitz Meadow. Go right and climb a series of stone steps for a few hundred yards. Reach a low ridge and follow the trail to the right, passing a number of campsites along the way, and in about a half mile, reach the Railroad Grade. It's a moraine in the shape of a giant half-pipe, a trough carved by the Easton Glacier as it slowly recedes up Mount Baker. (The glacier, by the way, is the source of Rocky Creek, the one you likely rock- and boulder-hopped early in this hike.) The trail follows the west rim in a smooth, consistent, uniform grade—almost like a railroad grade, hence the name.

Depending on the snow level, you can sometimes follow the trail and assorted snow-free spots up to an elevation of 7,000 feet. You may occasionally find yourself sidestepping marmots and expedition-pack-toting mountain climbers along the way; Railroad Grade is a popular approach route for folks climbing to Mount Baker's summit. But go only as far as the snow and your comfort level allow.

26 Scott Paul Trail

See map on page 103.

TYPE OF TRAIL: Hiking only.

TOTAL DISTANCE: 7.5-mile loop.

TIME REQUIRED: 5 hours.

DIFFICULTY LEVEL: Difficult.

ELEVATION GAIN: 1,800 feet.

MAPS: Green Trails Hamilton 45.

STARTING POINT: Go east on Highway 20 to just past milepost 82. Turn left onto Baker Lake Road and in about 12.2 miles, turn left onto Forest Service Road 12. In 3 miles, turn right onto Forest Service Road 13 and follow it for 6 miles to the road-end parking lot.

Trail runners on the Scott Paul Trail

THE HIKE: The trail is named for Scott Paul, a popular Forest Service employee who was tragically killed in a bridge-building accident.

This loop trail can be done in either direction. The following description follows the Park Butte and Railroad Grade trail descriptions (see Hikes 24 and 25) for about the first 2 miles. At the signed Scott Paul Trail intersection just below Morovitz Meadows (and the Railroad Grade Trail intersection), go right, and after passing through wildflower meadows, cross the lower reaches of the Easton Glacier moraine—that is, a rocky, bouldery stretch with rushing creeks but also awesome views to Mount Baker and particularly Sherman Peak, Baker's southside spire. Sherman Crater, just beyond, blew out in the mid-1800s and still steams to this day. A seasonal suspension bridge provides a way across the most rushing stretch of creek. (Check with the ranger beforehand at 360–856–5700 to make sure that the bridge is up.)

For about the next 3 miles, follow as the trail contours along the southern flank of Mount Baker—in and out of creek bends, but not much climbing—with sublime alpine views accompanying you the entire way. Mount Shuksan even makes an appearance. At about 5.5 miles from the trailhead, the trail re-enters forest and rambles downhill south through forest for about 2 miles until it rejoins the Park Butte and Railroad Grade Trails. Go left; the trailhead parking lot is about 100 yards away.

27 Dock Butte Trail

See map on page 101.

TYPE OF TRAIL: Hiking only.

TOTAL DISTANCE: 3.4 miles out-and-back.

TIME REQUIRED: 2 hours.

DIFFICULTY LEVEL: Difficult.

ELEVATION GAIN: 1,400 feet.

MAPS: Green Trails Hamilton 45.

STARTING POINT: Go east on Highway 20 to just past milepost 82. Turn left onto Baker Lake Road and in 12.2 miles, turn left onto Forest Service Road 12. Follow it for 6.8 miles (continuing straight at the intersection with Forest Service Road 13 at 3 miles) and turn left onto Forest Service Road 1230. Continue for 3.8 miles to the road-end trailhead.

THE HIKE: This trail begins at the same trailhead as the Blue Lake Trail (see Hike

23), but, unlike that one, doesn't get megacrowds. And if you're more of a panoramic mountain vista person than an alpine lake aficionado, the Dock Butte Trail will be more to your liking anyway. Views are so far-ranging from here, in fact, the butte is the site of a former lookout cabin, which burned down in 1964.

Hike the Blue Lake Trail for about a quarter mile to the signed intersection with the Dock Butte Trail. Go right and follow the trail as it steadily gains elevation through forest, past wildflower and heather meadows, and across a number of creeks and creeklets. In about a mile the trail begins a final steep, semiexposed push along a ridge to the summit of Dock Butte, which, at 5,239 feet, is just under a mile above sea level.

Views from here are spectacular—Mount Baker, only 8 air miles away, obviously has the lead, but also onstage are Mount Shuksan, the rusty Twin Sisters, and, far to the east, Eldorado Peak, the Picket Range, and the very heart of the North Cascades.

28 Baker Lake Trail–North Entrance

See map on pages 96–97.

TYPE OF TRAIL: Hiking, equestrian, llama packing.

TOTAL DISTANCE: 14.3 miles point-to-point.

TIME REQUIRED: 8 hours.

DIFFICULTY LEVEL: Moderate.

ELEVATION GAIN: 600 feet.

MAPS: Green Trails Lake Shannon 46.

STARTING POINT: Go east on Highway 20 to just past milepost 82, about 15 miles past Sedro-Woolley. Turn left onto Baker Lake Road. Continue for 26 miles to the road-end trailhead parking lot.

THE HIKE: This trail follows the shoreline of Baker Lake. However, the trail and several of its bridges sustained serious damage in fall 2003 due to flooding. Best to call the ranger before heading out to get the most up-to-date conditions.

The following description assumes you're doing a point-to-point hike, parking a car at both the north trailhead (the starting point described for this hike) and the south trailhead (see Hike 22 for Baker Lake Trail–South Entrance for directions). This description follows the trail from the north.

From the parking lot, follow the wide, barrier-free trail north 'twixt and 'tween giant cedars, along the Baker River. In a half mile or so, cross the cable-stay bridge to the right over the Baker River, following the sign for Baker Lake Trail. Once across, the barrier-free portion of trail ends, as the much narrower and sometimes overgrown trail heads south through denser, mossier, damper woods, with Baker River just to the right. The farther you go, the bigger the trees become, but don't expect to see Baker Lake again for a couple more miles.

Follow the trail, an old nineteenth-century lumbering and mining route, as it crosses (via bridges) Blum and Hidden Creeks, which, depending on runoff levels, can be quite exciting. And cold. The air above these and other creeks along the way feels 15 degrees cooler than the rest of the trail.

Baker Lake makes a return appearance at about 3 miles, just when the firs and cedars are starting to get really big. Mounts Baker and Shuksan views emerge, too, as do, depending on the lake level, the thousands of tree stumps at the bottom of the lake from when this valley was dammed in 1959 to create Baker Lake.

Reach the Noisy Creek Hiker Camp at about 4.5 miles from the trailhead. A great turnaround spot if you're not doing the whole trail, the camp is located to the right on a land finger jutting out into the lake and offers spectacular mountain and lake views, as well as a great place to dip your toes, enjoy a snack, and reenergize if you are continuing on. An interesting side trip is to follow the short, somewhat obscure Noisy Creek Trail across from the hiker camp, climbing steeply for about a quarter mile to what's known as the Noisy Creek Fir. It's almost 13 feet in diameter, 210 feet tall, and the sixth-largest Douglas fir tree in the world.

Back on the main trail, keep heading south, the lake always on your right, the hillside always on your left, and spectacular forest all around. In another 5 miles, you'll reach Maple Grove Camp, and Anderson Point Camp 2 miles beyond that. The south trailhead is about 2 miles farther south.

29 Anderson-Watson Lakes Trail

TYPE OF TRAIL: Hiking only.

TOTAL DISTANCE: 4 miles out-and-back for Anderson Lakes; 5 miles out-and-back for Watson Lakes.

TIME REQUIRED: 2 to 3 hours.

DIFFICULTY LEVEL: Moderate.

ELEVATION GAIN: 1,000 feet.

MAPS: Green Trails Lake Shannon 46.

STARTING POINT: Go east on Highway 20 to just past milepost 82, about

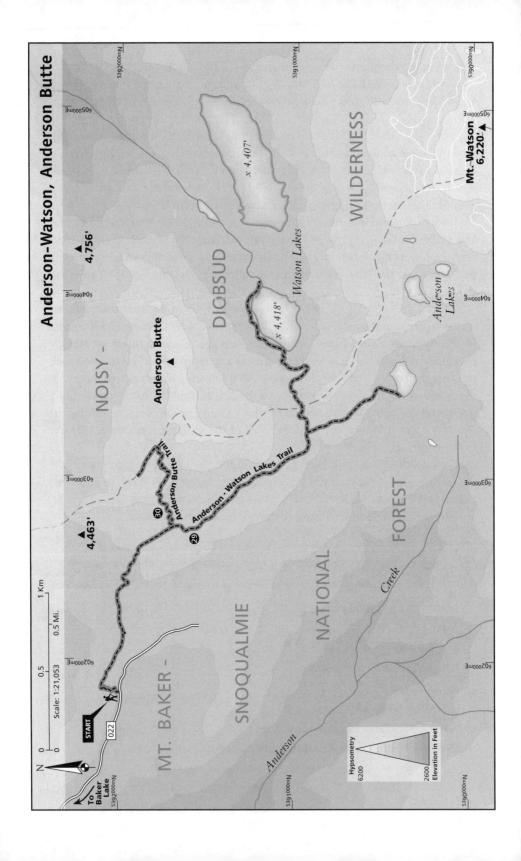

Anderson-Watson, Anderson Butte

N

Scale: 1:21,053

0   0.5   1 Km

0   0.5 Mi.

To Baker Lake

START

022

MT. BAKER -

SNOQUALMIE

NATIONAL

FOREST

Anderson Creek

Hypsometry

6200

2600

Elevation in Feet

NOISY -

DIOBSUD

WILDERNESS

Anderson Butte

Anderson Butte Trail

Anderson - Watson Lakes Trail

▲ 4,463'

29

30

▲ 4,756'

x 4,407'

x 4,418'

Watson Lakes

Anderson Lakes

Mt. Watson
6,220' ▲

5392000mN

6Q5000mE

6Q4000mE

6Q3000mE

6Q2000mE

5392000mN

5391000mN

5390000mN

6Q2000mE

6Q3000mE

6Q4000mE

6Q5000mE

15 miles past Sedro-Woolley. Turn left onto Baker Lake Road. At milepost 13.8, turn right onto gravel Forest Service Road 1106 (Baker Lake Dam Road). Cross Baker Dam in 1.8 miles. Just across, the road becomes Forest Service Road 1107. Follow it for 9 miles, then turn left onto Forest Service Road 022 and follow the sign for Watson Lakes Trail. The road-end trailhead is 1.1 miles ahead.

THE HIKE: Note the use of the plural in the trail heading, Anderson-Watson Lakes. That's because there are two Watsons (I presume) and several Andersons, though only one is really easy to get to. All of these alpine lakes are relatively easy to get to, are popular with families (many of whom come with the prerequisite galumphing, crotch-sniffing Labrador retriever), and allow fishing as long as you have a Washington State fishing license—all of which adds up to one thing: crowds. If you want privacy up here, visit during weekdays. Still, these sparkling lakes in a magical alpine setting are more than worthy of a visit.

From the trailhead, climb steadily through heavy timber for about a mile before entering lush, open, wildflower-goin'-crazy meadows. At the signed intersection just ahead, go right; a left leads to Anderson Butte (see Hike 30), a steep half-mile jaunt that leads to awesome views at the site of a former fire lookout station.

The trail gently roller-coasters up and down the mountain meadow for the next half mile or so, reenters the forest, and descends steeply for a couple hundred yards. Once back in the open, a signed intersection offers a couple choices: straight for Watson Lakes, right for Anderson.

Because the Watson Lakes have a more dramatic setting—open vistas to the surrounding peaks, which are numerous—and are bigger, with many opportunities for lakeside campsites, they're more popular. Head straight if the Watson Lakes are your destination.

After a short, semisteep forested climb to a saddle that rewards with open views down to the lakes, descend rather quickly into the lake basin. Reach the first Watson Lake, the smaller of the two, in about a mile. To reach the second lake, which has a more significant shoreline and stunning views up to Mount Watson, bear left (north) around the first lake; the second is just a few hundred yards beyond the first.

For Anderson Lakes, go right at the previous signed intersection. Reach the lake after about a half-mile mix of meadow and boulder field. With not quite the vistas of Watson Lakes, the main Anderson Lake is close enough to make for a quick side trip on the way to Watson.

30 Anderson Butte

See map on page 112.

TYPE OF TRAIL: Hiking only.

TOTAL DISTANCE: 3 miles out-and-back.

TIME REQUIRED: 2 hours.

DIFFICULTY LEVEL: Moderately difficult.

ELEVATION GAIN: 1,200 feet.

MAPS: Green Trails Lake Shannon 46.

STARTING POINT: Go east on Highway 20 to just past milepost 82, about 15 miles past Sedro-Woolley. Turn left onto Baker Lake Road. At milepost 13.8, turn right onto gravel Forest Service Road 1106 (Baker Lake Dam Road). Cross Baker Dam in about 1.5 miles, and in 0.6 mile past that, turn left onto Forest Service Road 1107. Follow it for 9 miles and turn left onto Forest Service Road 022 and follow the sign for Watson Lakes Trail. The road-end trailhead is 1.1 miles ahead.

THE HIKE: Not able to resist a play on the word *butte*, I'll say this short trail to the site of a former lookout station is a real *beaut*. The cabin, built in the 1930s and removed in 1964, might be long gone, but the reason it was built there in the first place—the site's open views to a stunning array of peaks and valleys—is certainly still there.

Accessed from the same trailhead as Anderson-Watson Lakes (see Hike 29), the route to Anderson Butte follows the same trail for the first mile. At a signed intersection at about 1 mile, just after the trail exits the forest, go left, following the sign for Anderson Butte.

The trail climbs steeply—about 600 feet over the next half mile—but not for long. A little less than 1.5 miles from the trailhead, reach a saddle, which immediately pays off with stunning views to the east. There's Mount Shuksan, the Pickets, Bacon Peak in the foreground, and lots more.

Follow the ridgeline trail to the left for a few hundred yards—to the point where another step would result in a fall of several hundred feet—and the former lookout site. The 360-degree views include the previously mentioned peaks as well as Mount Baker, the Twin Sisters, and, far down in the valley below, Baker Lake. Have some lunch and enjoy the views.

31 Shannon Ridge Trail

TYPE OF TRAIL: Hiking only.

TOTAL DISTANCE: 6 miles out-and-back.

TIME REQUIRED: 3 hours.

DIFFICULTY LEVEL: Difficult.

ELEVATION GAIN: 2,200 feet.

MAPS: Green Trails Mount Shuksan 14 (though the trail is not shown).

STARTING POINT: Go east on Highway 20 to just past milepost 82, about 15 miles past Sedro-Woolley. Turn left onto Baker Lake Road. Continue for 23.5 miles and turn left onto Forest Service Road 1152. Follow it for about 4 miles to Forest Service Road 1152-014 and turn right. In 1.5 miles, reach the road-end trailhead.

THE HIKE: This trail is mostly a climbers' route (read: *rough*) for those heading to the summit of Mount Shuksan via the Sulphide Glacier Route (see the Mountain Climbing section later in this chapter). Still, it gets up into some spectacular meadows with awesome views of Mount Baker, its Cascade brethren, and Baker Lake. (Oddly enough, it has only pretty good views of Mount Shuksan.) As a climbers' route the trail doesn't receive a whole lot of TLC and can be overgrown and, in places, hard to follow.

From the trailhead, the route follows a former logging road as it climbs gradually through an old clear-cut. At about 1.5 miles, the word *gradually* is left behind, as the trail switchbacks and scrambles steeply in old-growth forest for about a mile. Darkness abounds on even the sunniest days, but once the trail leaps out of the forest onto Shannon Ridge, all is lightness again, and the views extend for miles. The grade lessens, too, and the ridge invites about another half to three-quarters of a mile of wandering before you enter more rugged, climbers' country.

The North Cascades National Park boundary is about a half mile along the ridge. National Park Service wilderness backcountry permits are required for overnight stays in the park.

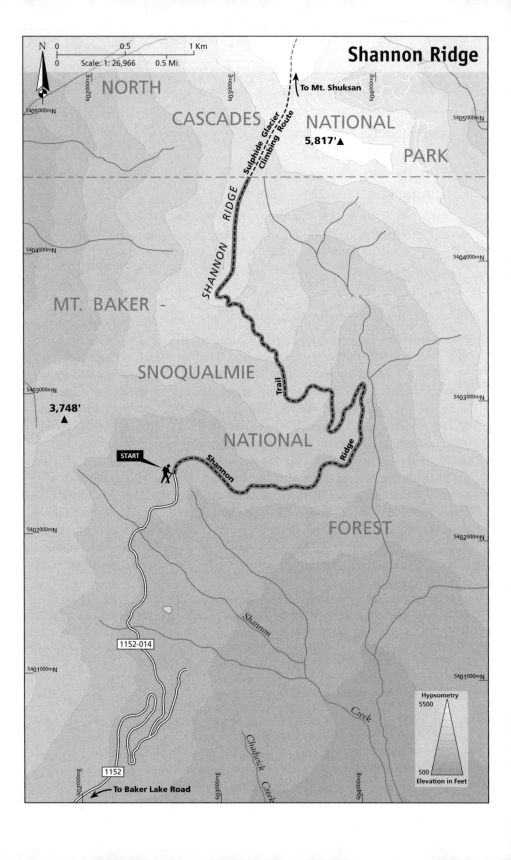

32 Sauk Mountain Trail

TYPE OF TRAIL: Hiking only.

TOTAL DISTANCE: 4.2 miles out-and-back.

TIME REQUIRED: 2 hours.

DIFFICULTY LEVEL: Moderately difficult.

ELEVATION GAIN: 1,200 feet.

MAPS: Green Trails Lake Shannon 46.

STARTING POINT: Go east on Highway 20 to milepost 96, about 7 miles east of Concrete, 29 miles east of Sedro-Woolley. Turn left onto Sauk Mountain Road (Forest Service Road 1030) and follow it for 7.5 steep, switchbacking miles to a fork. Go right onto sometimes-marked Forest Service Road 1036 and follow it for about a quarter mile to the end.

THE HIKE: All right, so maybe this one isn't exactly in the Mount Baker–Mount Shuksan region as described so far in this book, but it's got three things going for it. One, it's just outside the described area; two, it's not too difficult and fairly short; and three, most important, it offers spectacular views almost the entire way. And one more thing, because this trail is south-facing, it's always the first or one of the first mountain trails in the area to be free of snow.

From the parking lot, crane your neck for a gander up the broad open slope rising about 1,000 feet almost directly above you. Note the trail that switches back and forth and back and forth as it climbs. That's where you're headed, but rest assured, rewards are ample the entire way.

To the south, the all-encompassing views include the confluence of the Sauk and Skagit Rivers in a valley floor that, in prehistoric times, was the bottom of a massive lake dammed by glacial debris near present-day Concrete. To the east lay the heart of the North Cascades, and likely in the broad meadow surrounding you, wildflowers, wildflowers, and more wildflowers—among them, Indian paintbrush, phlox, tiger lilies, columbine, and lupine. On the clearest of days, Mount Rainier, almost 120 miles to the south, is visible.

About 1.5 miles from the trailhead, just after rounding a shoulder, reach a sometimes-signed intersection. Go left and continue climbing for a little more than a half mile to the site of a former lookout, which was removed in the early 1980s. Views improve and expand with each step—along with Mounts Baker and Shuksan, Puget Sound and the San Juan Islands are encompassed in the 360-degree vista.

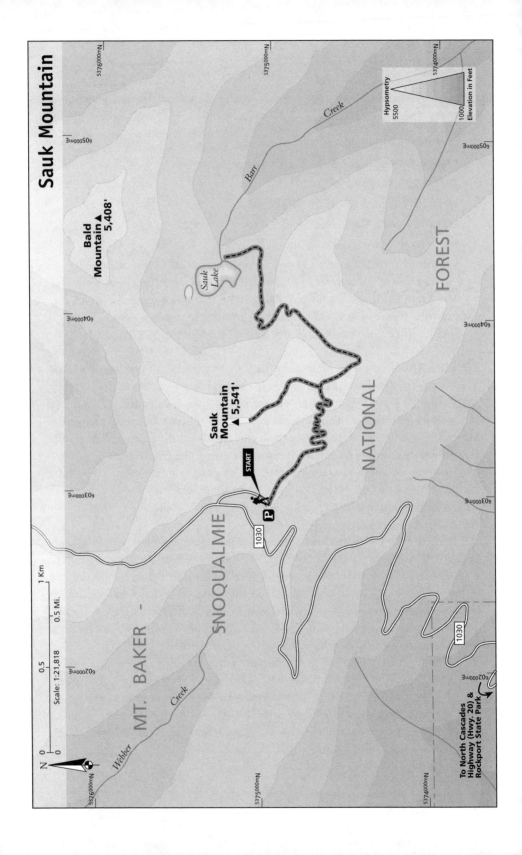

A right at the previous intersection leads down about 1,000 feet in 1.5 miles to Sauk Lake. Fishing is allowed (with a Washington State fishing license), as is camping at established campsites.

33 Cascade Trail

TYPE OF TRAIL: Hiker, biker, equestrian.

TOTAL DISTANCE: 22.3 miles one way.

TIME REQUIRED: Varies, depending on how much of it you hike.

DIFFICULTY LEVEL: Easy.

ELEVATION GAIN: Minimal.

MAPS: Trail is not on maps yet; check the Web site at www.skagitparks foundation.org.

STARTING POINT: This 22-mile rail trail that parallels Highway 20 from Sedro-Woolley to Concrete has numerous access points. Here are three main ones:

• *Fruitdale Road and Highway 20, Sedro-Woolley.* The parking lot is on the south side of the highway, about a half mile past the intersection of Highways 20 and 9.

• *Baker Lake Road and Highway 20.* The parking lot is on the left (north) side of Highway 20 just before the intersection with Baker Lake Road.

• *Concrete Senior Center.* Just past Silo Park in Concrete, at about Highway 20 milepost 88.5, turn left onto E Avenue and then right onto Railroad Street. The center's parking lot is just ahead at the end of the street.

THE HIKE: Here's another trail that's just outside the scope of this book but because of its unique recreation opportunities and history is worth including. From Sedro-Woolley, the trail passes through flats, farmland, and forest, and at times it hugs the Skagit River on its way to the town of Concrete (former name: Cement City), made famous in Tobias Wolfe's novel, *This Boy's Life.*

Because the trail follows an old rail line, the grade is never more than 1 or 2 percent, and inclines are just about imperceptible. The trail is about 70 feet above sea level in Sedro-Woolley, about 230 feet above sea level in Concrete. This low elevation ensures that the trail is usable pretty much year-round. And since it's built on railroad ballast, it drains especially well; there aren't a lot of muddy spots. Trail users often spot bald eagles, great blue herons, and, in an 80-acre corridor of preserved land about 4 miles west of Concrete, up to sixty elk that call the area home. Locals refer to this area as "Elk Meadows."

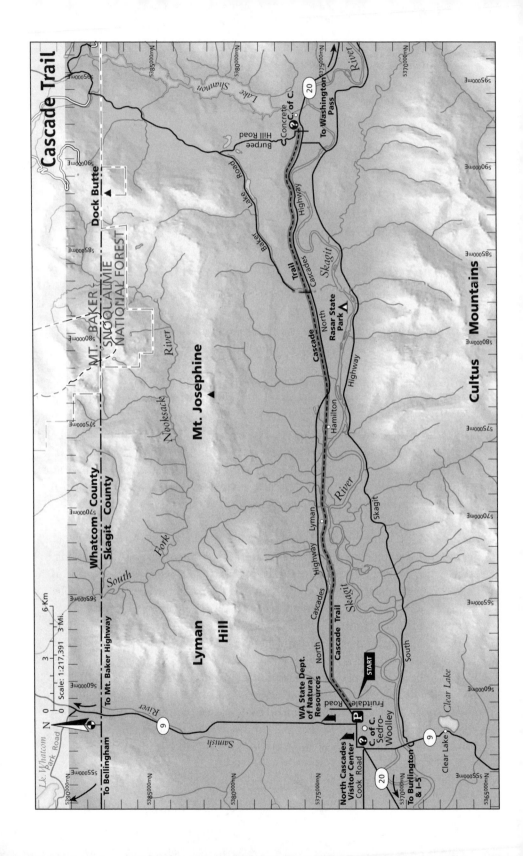

Cascade Trail

In 1993 Skagit County Parks purchased the rail corridor from the Burlington Northern Railroad and began transforming it into a trail for nonmotorized use, but not all Skagit County residents were pleased. Certain locals thought the land should be returned to those who owned it before the railroad. An organization to fight the trail, Citizens Against Rails to Trails (CART), sprang up. To this day at several points on private property adjacent to the trail, large signs denounce the trail as SKAGIT COUNTY'S PATH OF CORRUPTION and CORRIDOR LAND STOLEN BY SKAGIT COUNTY.

The corridor is being "railbanked," however. That means that if Burlington Northern decides in the future it wants to use the land as a rail line again, it can purchase the land back from the county, and thus ownership doesn't revert to the previous owner. In the interim the land can be used only as a nonmotorized trail. Throughout the 1990s much controversy surrounded the trail, but most of that has since died down.

Upper Baker Dam

Accessible Wilderness

A number of places in the Mount Baker–Mount Shuksan area are barrier-free and offer a wilderness experience to everyone. They're accessible not just for wheelchairs but also strollers and other wheeled vehicles. The following is a list of trails, day-use picnic areas, and vista points accessible to all. *(Note:* For information on campgrounds with accessible campsites, see the Camping section later in this chapter.)

Baker Lake Dam, Forest Service Road 1106, off Baker Lake Road MP 13.7: Though there are no visitor tours or interpretive center here (that's down in the town of Concrete), the Baker Lake Dam (officially, the Upper Baker Dam; the Lower Baker Dam is at the south end of Lake Shannon near Concrete) makes for an interesting stop. More than 300 feet high, the dam produces more than 100,000 kilowatts of power—*zowee!*—and helps provide flood control.

From Baker Lake Road, go right onto FR 1106 for 1.8 miles to the dam. A one-lane road crosses the top of the dam. Park on the near or far side of the dam (not *on* the dam itself), being sure to leave room for cars to get by.

Kulshan Campground, Forest Service Road 1106, off Baker Lake Road MP 13.7: Located about a half mile before the dam, Kulshan Campground offers several picnic spots and, at its north end by the boat launch, great views of Baker Lake. A short, rough road leads about a quarter mile to a lake and mountain viewpoint that includes Baker Lake Dam. From Baker Lake Road, follow FR 1106 for 1.3 miles to the campground, which will be on your left.

Shadow of the Sentinels Trail, Baker Lake Road MP 14.5: This wide pavement and boardwalk path offers a tour through a small-scale rain forest with moss- and lichen-hung trees 500 years old and older. Interpretive signs add to the experience. (See Hike 20 for a complete description.) *Note:* A Northwest Forest Pass is required to park at the trailhead.

Horseshoe Cove Campground Picnic Area, Baker Lake Road MP 15.2: With picnic benches right on the lake, this picnic spot provides an awesome setting for lunching or just munching in general. At milepost 15.2, go right onto Forest Service Road 1168 and follow it for 2 miles to the campground.

Panorama Point Campground Picnic Area, Baker Lake Road MP 19.3: The name says it best, and fortunately this picnic site is located right on the lake to take advantage of those panoramic views. Enjoy double vision—Mounts Baker and Blum and their reflections in the lake. Go right at milepost 19.3; the campground is right there.

Baker Lake Resort, Baker Lake Road MP 20.0: Along with lakefront picnic tables, the resort has the only store around. So if you forget the picnic basket, no problem. At milepost 20.0 go right and enter the resort. A day-use vehicle fee ($5.00) is required.

Shannon Creek Campground Picnic Area, Baker Lake Road MP 23.5: This small (two tables) day-use area at water's edge provides spectacular north-end Baker Lake views. Go right at milepost 23.5; the campground is straight ahead.

Worth Stopping

Puget Sound Energy Baker River Visitor Center, Highway 20 MP 89.5: Interpretive displays detail the story of not only the Upper and Lower Baker Lake Dams and the energy generated therein but also of the area salmon and their journey from Baker Lake to the Pacific Ocean and back. Smolts (young salmon) are actually removed from the lake and transported by truck (aka the "fish taxi") around the dams and released at the confluence of the Baker and Skagit Rivers. From there they make for Puget Sound and eventually the Pacific Ocean. In a few years, when it's time to spawn, the fish head back to the Skagit and Baker Rivers, where they once again hitch a taxi ride, this time back to Baker Lake Dam where they lay and fertilize their eggs.

From Highway 20 go left onto Everett Avenue for about a half mile. The visitor center is on your left.

Rockport State Park, Highway 20 MP 96.5: On even the brightest days, don't expect a lot of sun at this park's picnic area. But with good reason. The park's dense forest of 500-year-old Douglas fir trees—some 250 feet high—does its best to keep the sun from hitting the forest floor. Interpretive displays tell the story of Scottish naturalist David Douglas for whom these trees are named.

The park is 7 miles east of Concrete, just past Sauk Mountain Road on the left (north) side of the road. (*Note:* Because this is a Washington State park, a $5.00 day-use fee is required.)

Rasar State Park, Highway 20 MP 80.8: Along with a picnic area that features a shelter with kitchen facilities, this palindromic park boasts a quarter-mile paved trail to the Skagit River. Scan the sky and trees for eagles, especially in fall and winter. From milepost 80.8, about 1.5 miles east of Baker Lake Road, go right onto Lusk Road, then left onto Cape Horn Road to the end. The state-regulated $5.00 day-use fee is required here, too.

Photography

Looking for the best places to capture the Baker Lake basin on film or disk? Here are some suggestions.

For photographs of:	Go to:
Mount Baker	Park Butte Trail, Railroad Grade Trail, Dock Butte Trail
Mount Shuksan	Anderson Butte

Glaciers	Railroad Grade Trail
Ancient forest	Shadow of the Sentinels, Baker Lake (south end), Rockport State Park
Alpine lakes	Watson Lakes, Blue Lake
Wildflower meadows	Park Butte Trail, Railroad Grade Trail
Baker Lake and mountain backdrop	Panorama Point
Wild and scenic river	Rasar State Park
Eagles	Howard Miller Steelhead Park, North Cascades Highway MP 100

Camping

When it comes to sleeping out under the stars off Baker Lake Road, there are several ways to go: established Forest Service and Puget Sound Energy campgrounds that offer fire pits, pit toilets, and possibly running water (Forest Service campgrounds have no hookups; Puget Sound Energy ones do) and take reservations; primitive campsites along the Baker River at the north end of Baker Lake Road and along Baker Lake's east bank, accessed via Baker Lake Trail; hiker campsites located at certain trailheads; and backcountry camping and backpacking, which is free and requires only that you respect the land and your fellow campers. In addition, there are several lakeside pullout primitive camping spots along the last 6 miles of Baker Lake Road.

Developed Campgrounds

The following are developed campgrounds and, unless otherwise noted, are managed by the Forest Service. To reserve a spot at Horseshoe Cove, Boulder Creek, Panorama Point, Park Creek, or Shannon Creek Campgrounds, call (877) 444–6777 or visit the Web site at www.reserveusa.com. To reserve a site at Kulshan Campground or Baker Lake Resort, call (888) 711–3033.

Kulshan Campground: This posh, 100-plus site campground is managed by Puget Sound Energy, the same folks who brought you Baker Lake. You'll luxuriate in flush toilets (Kulshan is one of only two of the six lakeside campgrounds to have them), running water, full hookups, boat ramp, and water access with great views across the lake to Mount Shuksan. The only drawback is that at press time, there were no wheelchair-accessible campsites.

To get here, go east on Highway 20 to just past milepost 82. Turn left onto Baker Lake Road. At milepost 13.8, turn right onto gravel Forest Service Road

1106 (Baker Lake Dam Road) and follow it for 1.3 miles to Kulshan Campground on the left.

Baker Dam is just a half mile east, and the Baker Lake Trail–South Entrance about another half mile beyond that. Forest Service Road 12, the access road to Schreibers Meadow and the Mount Baker National Recreation Area, is 2.8 miles south.

Horseshoe Cove Campground: Five campgrounds managed by the Forest Service line the west shores of Baker Lake, and Horseshoe Cove is the first one you come to, a little less than 16 miles along Baker Lake Road. The campground features a boat ramp, swimming area, and three group sites for up to twenty-five people each. About twenty of the thirty-four sites can be reserved; the rest are available on a first-come, first-served basis. Three sites are wheelchair accessible. Horseshoe Cove also features pit toilets and running water. This campground is open from the end of May through early October. To get here, go north on Baker Lake Road to milepost 15.2 and turn right onto Forest Service Road 1168. Continue for about 2 miles into the campground.

Nearby trails include Shadow of the Sentinels (see Hike 20) about three-quarters of a mile south of FR 1168 on Baker Lake Road, and Boulder Ridge Trail, whose access road is a little more than 3 miles north. Forest Service Road 12, the access road to Schreibers Meadow and the Mount Baker National Recreation Area, is about 3 miles south.

Boulder Creek Campground: One of two lake campgrounds not actually on the lake, Boulder Creek is the smallest and most primitive. It has only eight sites, five of which can be reserved, and unfortunately none are wheelchair accessible. There's no running water per se, though since all sites are pretty much creekside, that's kind of like running water. Boulder Creek Campground is open from the end of May through early September. To get here, go north on Baker Lake Road to milepost 17.9 and turn right into the campground.

Forest Service Road 1130, the access road to the Boulder Ridge Trail, is about a quarter mile north. The Baker River and Baker Lake–North Entrance Trails can be accessed about 8 miles north at the end of Baker Lake Road. Forest Service Road 12, the access road to Schreibers Meadow and the Mount Baker National Recreation Area, is a little less than 6 miles south.

Panorama Point Campground: As the name implies, Panorama Point is big on views, situated as it is on a nubbin of land that juts out into the lake. Several lakeside sites are available and, not surprisingly, are very popular. Nine of the campground's fifteen tent and trailer sites (which include two wheelchair-accessible ones) can be reserved. Along with vault toilets and water, the campground has a boat launch area. The campground is open from late May through early October. To get here, go north on Baker Lake Road to milepost 19.3 and turn right into the campground.

Nearby hiking trails include the Boulder Ridge Trail, accessed about a mile south of Panorama Point Campground, and the Baker River and Baker Lake–North Entrance Trails, located about 7 miles north at the end of Baker Lake Road. Forest Service Road 12, the access road to Schreibers Meadow and the Mount Baker National Recreation Area, is about 7 miles south.

Baker Lake Resort: Owned by Puget Sound Energy, this laid-back lake-front compound has ninety campsites (some with full hookups), nine cabins, a playground, a boat launch with kayak rentals, great lakefront views (of course), and the only store in the area. Unfortunately, none of the sites are wheelchair accessible.

Since PSE acquired the property in the late 1990s, it has been slowly renovating and refurbishing the resort, which is open from early May through early October. To get here, go north on Baker Lake Road to milepost 20.0 and turn right into the campground and resort.

Park Creek Campground is just across Baker Lake Road, and nearby hiking trails include the Boulder Ridge Trail, accessed via Forest Service Road 1130, about 2 miles south, and the Baker River and Baker Lake–North Entrance Trails, located about 6 miles north at the end of Baker Lake Road. Forest Service Road 12, the access road to Schreibers Meadow and the Mount Baker National Recreation Area, is about 8 miles south.

Park Creek Campground: Just across the road from Baker Lake Resort, this is the other nonlakeside campground in the Baker Lake basin. Like Boulder Creek, this one is a tad primitive. No running water or vault toilets, but plenty of what camping is really for in the first place—peace and quiet. Seven of the wooded campground's sites can be reserved, but none are wheelchair accessible. Park Creek is open from late May through early September. To get here, go north on Baker Lake Road to milepost 20.0 and turn left into the campground. It's directly across the road from Baker Lake Resort.

Nearby hiking trails include the Boulder Ridge Trail, accessed via Forest Service Road 1130, about 2 miles south, and the Baker River and Baker Lake–North Entrance Trails, located about 6 miles north at the end of Baker Lake Road. Forest Service Road 12, the access road to Schreibers Meadow and the Mount Baker National Recreation Area, is about 8 miles south.

Shannon Creek Campground: The farthest north of the Baker Lake Campgrounds, Shannon Creek offers twenty sites, of which eleven can be reserved. Located right on the lake, the campground has a boat ramp, swimming area, and running water. Only one wheelchair-accessible site is available. The campground is open from late May through early October. To get here, go north on Baker Lake Road to milepost 23.5 and turn right into the campground.

Nearby hiking trails are Baker River and Baker Lake–North Entrance Trails; the trailhead for both is 2.5 miles north at the end of Baker Lake Road.

Baker Lake Resort dock

Forest Service Road 12, the access road to Schreibers Meadow and the Mount Baker National Recreation Area, is about 11 miles south.

Rockport State Park: This 670-acre camping park is located about 16 miles east of the area covered in this book but is included because of its camping and recreation opportunities—and its trees. The park is situated in the midst of an ancient forest of Douglas firs that have never been logged, highly unusual for this lowland area. The canopy is so dense that on even the sunniest bluebird days, you're almost always in the shade. Just across Highway 20 is the Skagit River, a nationally designated wild and scenic area and winter home to more than 400 bald eagles that come from all over the Northwest for the good eats.

The park features sixty campsites (all first-come, first-served), including a group site for up to forty-five people, restrooms with flush toilets, showers, hookups, and 5 miles of hiking trails. There are two ADA-accessible sites. For those who want some of the comforts of home, Rockport makes a great base for exploring the Baker Lake area.

To get to Rockport State Park, head east on Highway 20 to milepost 96.5, about 14 miles east of Baker Lake Road and 7 miles east of Concrete. The well-signed park is on the left (north). The Sauk Mountain Trail (see Hike 32) is about a half mile west of the park.

For information, call the park directly at (360) 853–8461 or call Washington State Parks at (360) 902–8844. Or check online at www.parks.wa.gov and go to Park Information.

Rasar State Park: This newish, forty-site camping park, a mile from Baker Lake Road, has hookups, playground, Skagit River access, and trails. The park has two ADA-accessible campsites. This is also the only Washington State park that's a palindrome; that is, spelled the same backward and forward.) To get there, head east on Highway 20 to milepost 80.8, about 1.5 miles east of Baker Lake Road. Go right onto Lusk Road, then left onto Cape Horn Road to the end. For more information, call (360) 826–3942 or check online at www.parks .wa.gov and go to Park Information.

Hiker Sites

In the Baker Lake basin, a few trailhead hiker camps are available for those interested in getting an early start, whether it be for climbing, hiking, or backpacking. These camps are located at Schreibers Meadow, the trailhead for Park Butte, along with the Railroad Grade and Scott Paul Trails (see Hikes 25 and 26), and at the end of Baker Lake Road at the Baker River and Baker Lake–North Entrance Trailhead.

Baker Lake Camping: Along the 14-mile-long Baker Lake Trail, there are four primitive campgrounds and hiker camps on the east bank that offer tent sites only. They're available on a first-come, first-served basis and are true pack-it-in, pack-it-out sites. Most people access the campgrounds via the Baker Lake Trail, but the grounds are also popular for canoe- and kayak-camping destinations. From south to north, here's where to find the following camping areas.

- Anderson Point: 1.8 miles
- Maple Grove (the most "established" campground, with picnic tables and fire grills): 3.8 miles
- Silver Creek: 7.3 miles
- Noisy Creek: 8.8 miles

Taking in Baker River

Backcountry Camping

Overnight camping is permitted on most of the Forest Service trails in the Baker Lake area. Remember to set up tents in established campsites or on rock, snow, or bare ground. Please try not to walk on heather and other vegetation, which at alpine and subalpine levels have a short growing season. Practice zero-impact camping. Open fires are prohibited in national park, wilderness, and national recreation areas.

Here's information on camping on individual trails.

Anderson-Watson Lakes Trail: Several marked campsites along both Watson Lakes.

Baker Lake Trail: See the previous Hiker Sites section for information on several primitive camping areas along the trail.

Baker River Trail: Sulphide Camp, with several campsites, is located on the banks of Sulphide Creek at the end of the trail. Because the trail enters North Cascades National Park about a mile before the camp, a wilderness permit is required for overnight stays. The permit can be obtained at the National Park Service offices in Sedro-Woolley.

Blue Lake Trail: Established campsites can be found at the lake.

Park Butte Trail: Designated campsites can be found at the trailhead at Schreibers Meadow and on the trail at the base of Cathedral Crag, about a half mile past the intersection with the Railroad Grade Trail. The Park Butte Lookout, at the end of the trail, is also available for overnight stays on a first-come, first-served basis.

Railroad Grade Trail: Along with at the Schreibers Meadow Trailhead, some impossible-to-miss, designated tent pads can be found about a half mile from where the trail leaves the Park Butte Trail in Morovitz Meadow. (Camping is allowed anywhere above 6,000 feet, where it's all rock or snow anyway.)

Sauk Mountain Trail: Campsites are available near Sauk Lake. Access the lake via a spur trail that heads down and into the lake basin at about the 1.5-mile mark of the Sauk Mountain Trail.

Scott Paul Trail: Camping is available at the Schreibers Meadow Trailhead but nowhere along the trail.

Shannon Ridge Trail: Campsites can be found on the ridge starting at about 2.5 miles. About a half mile farther, the trail enters North Cascades National Park where a wilderness permit is required for overnight stays. These can be obtained at the National Park Service offices in Sedro-Woolley or Marblemount.

Backpacking

BP4 Baker Lake Trail

See map on pages 160–61.

The 14-mile Baker Lake Trail (see Hike 28), which hugs the east bank of Baker Lake (the trail was formerly known as the East Bank Trail), offers a point-to-point backpacking experience with the option of staying at one or more of the lakeside hiker camp areas (see the previous Hiker Sites section). Start at the north end so you get the perhaps slightly less fascinating, nonlakeside section out of the way first.

Another option: Turn the trip into a 28-mile out-and-back trip by turning around and heading back once you reach the end. In this case, for less driving, start and finish at the south end near Baker Lake (see Hike 22).

BP5 Scott Paul–Railroad Grade–Park Butte Trails

See map on pages 160–61.

This triumvirate of overlapping trails accessed at Schreibers Meadow can be linked together to make a 13- to 15-mile backpacking route, depending on how much exploration you want to do up the Railroad Grade Trail. (See Hikes 24, 25, and 26 for complete trail descriptions.) Start with the Scott Paul Trail, heading right into forest (the opposite direction from the description in the Day Hikes section) and eventually into the alpine country below Mount Baker's Squak Glacier.

Camping is not allowed on the Scott Paul, so wait to set up camp until you hit the Railroad Grade Trail, where there are many choices. After exploring the Easton Glacier environs, add the Park Butte Trail. If you're lucky and no one's already claimed it for the night, the Park Butte Lookout makes a cool overnight option.

Mountain Climbing

The most popular route to the summit of Mount Shuksan and the second-most popular route to the top of Mount Baker are accessed from this south-side Baker Lake basin area. Climbers heading for Baker via the Easton Glacier Route leave from the Schreibers Meadow area on the south side of the mountain and head up the Railroad Grade Trail (see Hike 25); Mount Shuksan's Sulphide Glacier Route is approached via the Shannon Ridge Trail (see Hike 31).

Most climbers take two days for a summit climb. On the first day they hike to the edge of the glacier, where they set up camp and go to sleep early so that they can start climbing at about 1:00 A.M. It's much safer to do the required six to nine hours of glacier climbing at night when the colder air ensures that the snow and glacier are more solid.

Permits are not required to climb Mounts Baker or Shuksan, though climbers are encouraged to sign the climbers' register at the national forest Mount Baker Ranger District and national park headquarters in Sedro-Woolley.

My words of caution about mountaineering earlier in this book apply here, too: It's a potentially dangerous activity, so it's your responsibility to use proper equipment and get glacier travel experience and training before you attempt any of the climbs mentioned below. Also, never forget that the weather can change rapidly at high altitudes; it can snow at any time 5,000 feet above and visibility can quickly be reduced to nothing.

A list of climbing guide services can be found in the Mountain Climbing and Scrambling section in the North Side section of this book.

C4 Mount Baker

Easton Glacier Route: Among the least technical climb of any of the Cascade volcanoes, and with easy access via the Schreibers Meadow area, the Easton

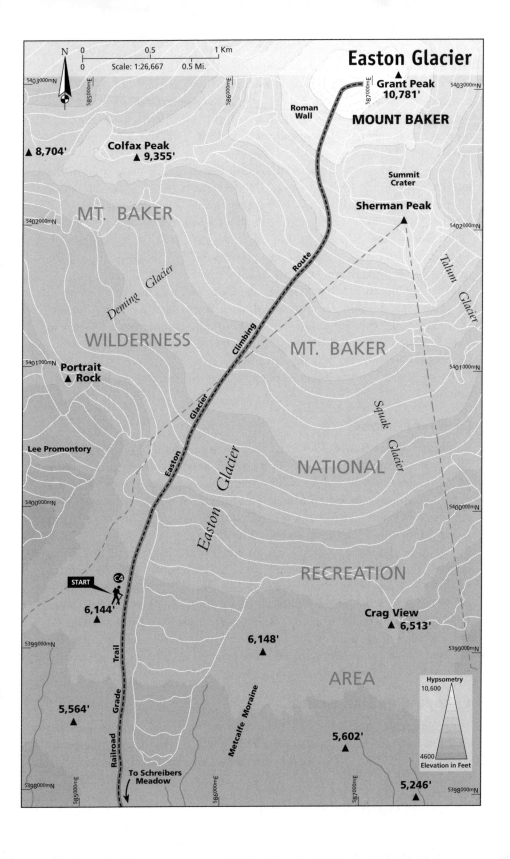

Glacier Route can be crowded on summer weekends. And in spring the experience can be dampened a tad by the whirring, whiny engines of snowmobiles that are allowed in the Mount Baker National Recreation Area, which the Easton Glacier Route passes through. That said, climbing Mount Baker from any route is a truly sublime, otherworldly experience that will stay with you for the rest of your life.

From the Schreibers Meadow Trailhead, hike the Park Butte Trail to the intersection with the Railroad Grade Trail (see Hikes 24 and 25) and follow it up the west rim of the Easton Glacier moraine. Keep climbing. And climbing. Camping spots can be found starting at about 5,600 feet on up to 7,000 feet. Depending on how high you want to carry your stuff, pick an appropriate spot, set up camp, have some chow, and then pretend you'll be able to go to sleep for the night, even though you know you'll have to wake up at midnight

After roping up, climbers head up the Easton Glacier in the direction of Sherman Peak, the pointy pyramid on Mount Baker's south shoulder. After several hours, a flat spot is reached at the base of this shoulder peak, adjacent to steaming Sherman Crater. It's an amazing geologic wonder but one whose sulfur odor might have you holding your nose.

From here it's a 1,000-foot, 30-degree push up the Roman Wall to the summit.

C5 Mount Shuksan

Sulphide Glacier Route: This is the least technical and most popular route to the summit of Mount Shuksan. Still, it requires several miles of glacier travel, which, given the potential for falling into deep crevasses, is not without a degree of risk. Also, scaling Mount Shuksan's final 600-foot rock pyramid requires rock-climbing skills and as such is a more technical climb than Mount Baker. Thus, only a brief description is offered here.

Access the Sulphide Glacier Route via the Shannon Ridge Trail. Follow the ridge north, and after crossing into North Cascades National Park, set up camp (national park overnight permit required). From the ridge continue north as the grade steepens, and at about 6,000 feet, step onto the Sulphide Glacier. (Some folks like to camp on the west edge of the glacier at about 6,500 feet.) Make for the obvious summit rock pyramid about 2.5 miles away, bearing to the left (west) as you go. Once there, the 600-foot pyramid itself offers several parallel rock gullies to the top. Most are class 3 and 4.

Canoeing and Kayaking

With spectacular, unobstructed views of Mounts Baker and Shuksan, paddling in Baker Lake can be a sublime experience—and at certain times of the year, a somewhat surreal one. The lake is a reservoir whose water level varies through-

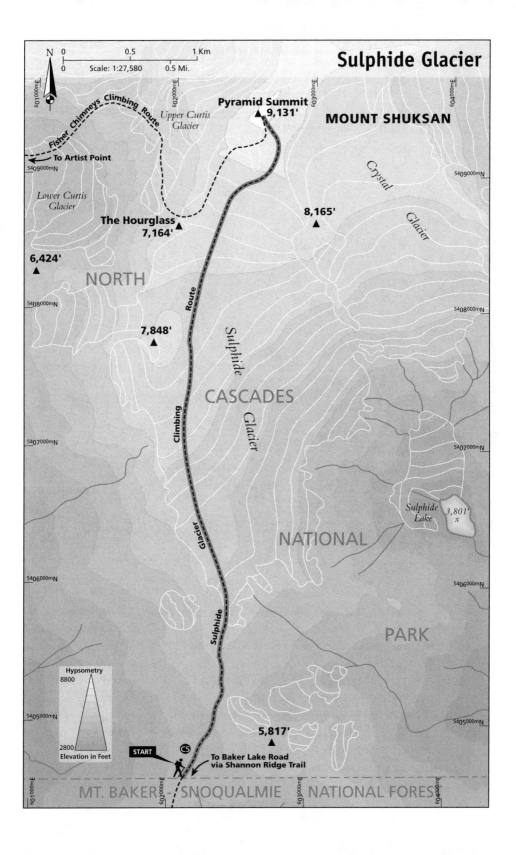

Kayaker paddling on Baker Lake with Mount Blum in the distance

out the year according to snowmelt, rain, and energy demand. Roughly speaking, the water level is lowered in fall and winter to allow for flood storage (i.e., room for excess rain and meltwater) and raised around Memorial Day for recreation purposes (i.e., boating). When the level is low, there are places where those stumps stick up or can be seen below the surface of the water.

Some think the best time of the year is after Labor Day when the crowds—that is, Jet Skis and motorboats—thin out considerably. But summer weekdays can be pretty sparse, too. If you don't have your own boat, Baker Lake Resort rents canoes, kayaks, paddleboats, and motorboats (see the entry in the Camping section earlier in this chapter).

As for where to put in, the following campgrounds offer boat ramps: Kulshan, Horseshoe Cove, Panorama Point, Baker Lake Resort, and Shannon Creek.

Interested in kayak or canoe camping? Paddle over to the east bank of Baker Lake, where a number of primitive campgrounds and campsites can be found. Roughly speaking, Anderson Point Camp is across the lake from Horseshoe Cove Campground; Maple Grove is about halfway between Horseshoe Cove and Boulder Creek; Silver Creek and Noisy Creek are across the lake between Baker Lake Resort and Shannon Creek.

Fishing

Baker Lake is a hotbed for the type of angling enthusiasts who like to ogle some sublime alpine scenery while waiting for the fish to bite, which means probably all anglers. Fishing for trout (rainbow, cutthroat, and bull) and kokanee (salmon that stay in lakes when other types of salmon make for the ocean) is good. Favorite methods include fly, spin, and bait. All seasons save for winter are good, with fall being the best. A Washington State fishing license is required. Fishing licenses cost just over $20 and are available through a number of local vendors including Red Apple Market and Cascade Supply in Concrete and Sports and More in Sedro-Woolley. They're also available online through the Washington Department of Fish and Wildlife Web site at www.wdfw.wa.gov.

Boat launches and lakeside campgrounds offer numerous spots for lake access.

Biking

Mountain Biking

As on the north side of the Mount Baker–Mount Shuksan area, there's unfortunately a dearth of mountain biking opportunities in the Baker Lake basin. No Forest Service or national park trails here allow bikes. They are allowed on Forest Service roads, and while many of these roads provide big climbs and breakneck descents, almost none of them offer open vistas except for short stretches. Still, there is a bit of interesting riding to be had. Here are some suggestions.

Forest Service Road 1106/Kulshan Campground: This road crosses along the top of Baker Lake Dam and offers some big-time views of the massive Puget Sound Energy structure that holds back the waters of Baker Lake. Park at Kulshan Campground and ride east for a half mile to the dam. Continue across to Forest Service Road 1107 until the grade becomes too much, or return to the campground and head for a nifty viewpoint overlooking the lake near the campground's boat launch. Various exploratory side roads head north for a short ways.

Forest Service Road 1107: For an epic ride wherein you can pretend that you're riding a Tour de France Alps stage, pedal the 10 miles from Kulshan Campground to the ridge just before the Anderson-Watson Lakes Trailhead (see Hike 29), climbing 3,500 feet. Or for less climbing but just as many views, drive 8.5 miles on FR 1107 (to the last switchback just before the turnoff for Forest Service Road 1107-022 and Anderson-Watson Lakes) and turn left onto FSR 1107-022. Park here on the side of the road. Views along this ridge are huge, especially of Mount Baker to the west and deep down into the Baker Lake basin.

FR 1107-022 continues north, gradually descending for about 2 miles; after that it drops steeply enough that you won't want to turn around and ride back up to your car.

A further riding option is to ride south on FSR 1107 past the turnoff for FR 1107-022 (the road to the Anderson-Watson Lakes Trailhead) for about 1.5 miles. You'll be rewarded with even more open Baker—lake and mountain— vistas.

Cascade Trail: From Sedro-Woolley to Concrete, this 22-mile, 14-foot-wide rail trail offers scenic riding through farmland and forest and, at points, along the Skagit River (see Hike 33). The trail climbs ever so slightly from a low of 70 feet above sea level in Sedro-Woolley to 230 feet in Concrete. During winter months the trail, while not muddy, can be a bit squishy in spots and hard to pedal.

Baker Lake Road: About the last 6 miles of Baker Lake are unpaved and mostly flat, and almost all of it hugs Baker Lake's shoreline, making for a nice ride. The only downside is that on summer weekends when there are lots of cars heading to and from campgrounds and trailheads along this stretch, it can become quite dusty.

Road Biking

Baker Lake Road: As the only paved road in the area covered in this book, Baker Lake Road is pretty much the only choice for road cycling. Though the road starts out at an elevation of about 200 feet and climbs to a high of about 1,100, most of the paved road adjacent to Baker Lake is between 700 and 1,100 feet above sea level. There are some sustained climbs and descents but nothing akin to riding the last 10 miles of the Mount Baker Highway, which climbs 3,000 feet on the way to Artist Point. *Note:* Be aware that cars sometimes drive Baker Lake Road at excessive speed with little regard for bicyclists.

Winter/Spring

Winter lasts a long time in the Mount Baker–Mount Shuksan area, and even when it's not winter any longer, its aftereffects (e.g., snow) linger for a long time after. At the higher elevations (above 4,000 feet), snow starts falling sometime in October, with the first significant dumps usually occurring in November. The Mount Baker Ski Area, which at 3,400 to 5,000 feet is a good barometer of where the snow level is, often opens by Thanksgiving. Though the ski area closes at the end of April, enough snow still remains that the last 3 miles of the Mount Baker Highway—from the ski area to Artist Point—aren't plowed free of snow until sometime in July (and then that stretch closes again in October when the snow begins falling.) The average annual snowfall at the ski area is 600 inches, the highest of any ski area in North America, with a world record of 1,140 inches falling during the 1998–1999 season.

North Side

The Mount Baker Ski Area is the number one destination in the area not just for those who want to ride the lifts up and slide the snow down, but also backcountry types for whom it's important to earn their turns, as well as families interested in free snow fun—i.e., tobogganing, snow tubing, and just playing around in general. That's because the paved Mount Baker Highway is plowed free of snow to Heather Meadows and the Mount Baker Ski Area; thus in winter and spring it's the easiest and safest access to the snowy alpine country.

Mount Baker Ski Area

When you get right down to it, Mount Baker is a fairly small ski area (1,000 acres, eight lifts, with only a 1,500-foot vertical) with nary a single high-speed quad, no shops or boutiques, no après-ski life, no nightlife to speak of, and not a single bed on which to spend the night. In fact, the closest accommodations are 19 miles down the hill in the small, blink-and-you'll-miss-it town of Glacier.

Yet the Mount Baker Ski Area is one of the most well-known winter playgrounds anywhere. In fact, while the ski area ranks fourth in Washington State in number of skier visits, as of 2004 it's ninth in the *world* when it comes to ski areas written about or photographed for ski and snowboard publications.

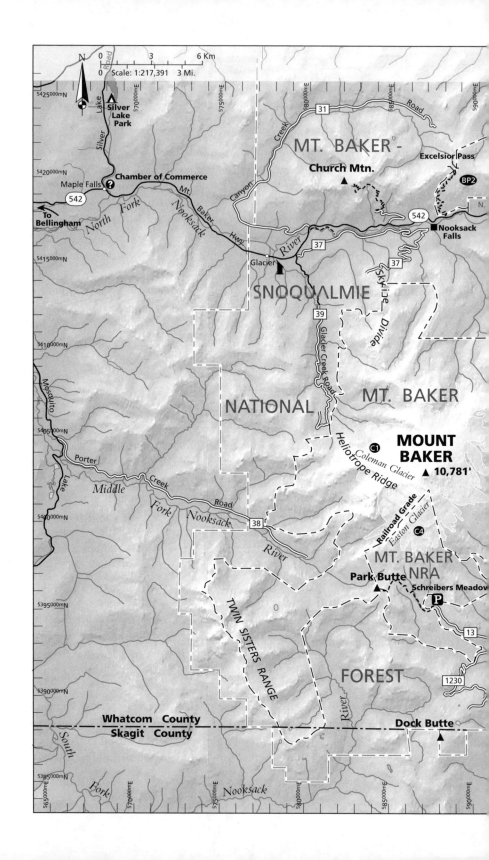

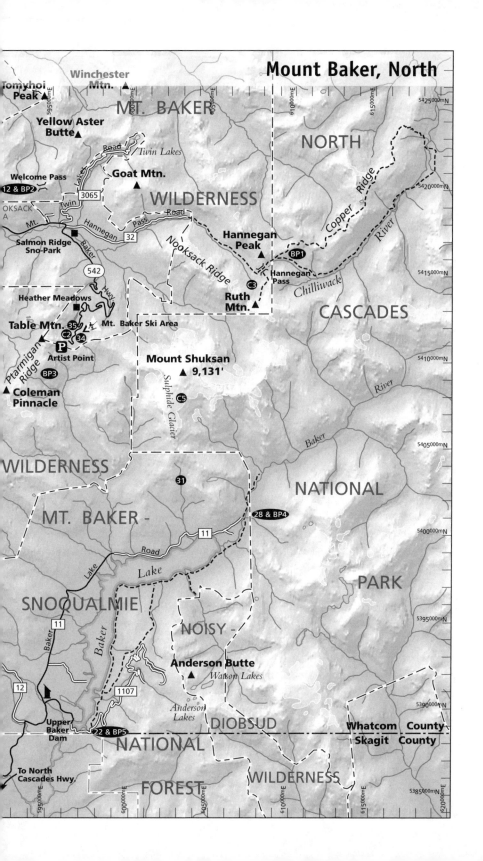

Tomyhoi Peak ▲

Winchester Mtn. ▲

MT. BAKER

NORTH

Yellow Aster Butte ▲

Twin Lakes

Road

Welcome Pass
12 & BP2

Goat Mtn. ▲

WILDERNESS

3065

OKSACK A

Twin

Mt.

Pass

Road

Hannegan

Baker

Nooksack Ridge

Hannegan Peak ▲

BP1

Copper Ridge

River

Salmon Ridge Sno-Park

32

C3

Hannegan Pass

Chilliwack

542

Hwy.

Ruth Mtn. ▲

CASCADES

Heather Meadows

Table Mtn. 85 ▲
C2 34
P
Artist Point

Mt. Baker Ski Area

Mount Shuksan
▲ **9,131'**

River

Ptarmigan Ridge
BP3

▲ **Coleman Pinnacle**

Sulphide Glacier

C5

River

Baker

5425000mN

5420000mN

5415000mN

5410000mN

5405000mN

WILDERNESS

31

NATIONAL

28 & BP4

MT. BAKER -

11

Road

Lake

Lake

5400000mN

PARK

5395000mN

SNOQUALMIE

11

Baker

Lake

Baker

NOISY -

Anderson Butte
▲ Watson Lakes

5390000mN

12

1107

Anderson Lakes

DIOBSUD

Whatcom County
Skagit County

Upper Baker Dam

22 & BP5

NATIONAL

To North Cascades Hwy.

FOREST

WILDERNESS

5385000mN

Avalanche Danger

Talk about snow brings up the issue of avalanche. The snow that falls in this part of the North Cascades is especially wet and heavy. Some call it "Cascade crud." Close to the ocean and on the west side of the Cascade Mountain Range, and with temperatures that rarely drop far below freezing (i.e., single digits or below zero), the snow that falls here is rarely the light, fluffy powder that falls on the east side of the Cascades or is typical of the Rocky Mountains. It's heavy and wet, piles up fast, and is prone to avalanche. Each year about thirty to thirty-five Americans die in avalanches, and unfortunately, the Mount Baker–Mount Shuksan area claims a disproportionately high number of avalanche victims. During the 1998–1999 record snowfall season, three of the nation's twenty-six avalanche fatalities occurred either within or just out of bounds at the Mount Baker Ski Area.

What follows are some tips on precautions to take and what to do if you plan to be traveling in avalanche country. Avalanches can occur at any time of year but are especially common in winter, spring, and early summer. (Keep in mind that whole courses are given in avalanche awareness and the science behind it all, and that the following tips are no substitute for avalanche training.)

- Check the Northwest Weather and Avalanche forecast Web site at http://www.nwac.noaa.gov or call the hotline at (206) 526-6677 for the latest conditions.

- Never travel alone.

- Along with the ten essentials—map, compass, flashlight or headlamp with extra batteries and bulb, extra food, extra clothing, water, sunglasses and sunscreen, pocketknife, matches in a waterproof container and fire starter, and first-aid kit—add these to your list for winter backcountry travel: avalanche transceiver and the knowledge to use it, ski or trekking poles, and a portable shovel.

- Do not cross below steep open slopes where avalanches have already occurred.

A number of factors contribute to the Mount Baker legend. One, its steep, deep terrain with naturally occurring half-pipes that look like waves frozen in snow. Two, its epic snowfall—600-plus inches per year, the most of any ski area in North America. Three, and perhaps most important, the decision way back in the early 1980s to allow a couple of teenagers who had only a single plank attached to their boots—the first snowboarders, they were—to ride the mountain.

- Don't blindly follow tracks in the snow assuming that those who've gone before you know an avalanche-safe route.
- Be aware that the most dangerous time for avalanches is during heavy snowfall (rates of 1 inch or more per hour) and warming periods with heavy rains or sunshine.
- Avoid traveling along valley bottoms below slopes you suspect may avalanche. Ridgetops are safer, though you need to watch out for overhanging cornices.
- Most slopes that avalanche are at angles of 30 to 45 degrees, roughly the same angle as slopes at ski areas and the more sought-after backcountry slopes. Be aware also that most avalanches occur on slopes that are steep north-, east-, or leeward-facing, or on south-facing slopes in the middle of the day.
- If you do find yourself caught in an avalanche, fight hard to keep from getting swept away. Try to grab onto anything—a rock, a tree—or dig your poles or ice ax into the snow to keep from being swept away. If that fails, try a swimming motion—flailing your arms and legs—in an attempt to stay at the surface of the slide. If your head goes below the surface of the snow, close your mouth, and as the slide stops, try to thrust upward. If buried, put your hand in front of your face to create breathing room. Remain calm, conserving energy and oxygen. As long as you weren't traveling alone, your chances of being found are good.
- If you have any doubt about whether your route is avalanche safe, cancel it or substitute it with a trip you know to be safe. Perhaps someplace with gentle, forested slopes, little snowpack, or both.
- Take an avalanche training course, one that teaches you to recognize slopes and snow types prone to avalanche and instructs you in the proper use of avalanche transceivers.

Soon the ski area's reputation grew as the first and only place where snowboarders were not just allowed but welcomed with open arms—general manager Duncan Howat took up the sport, as did his daughter Amy, who would go on to be a world champion—and Mount Baker became snowboarding's mecca, the fountainhead of slacker snowboarder cool.

The Legendary Banked Slalom—a snowboarding race down one of the ski area's natural half-pipes, first held in 1985—has brought further attention to

Slalom race at the Mount Baker Ski Area

the Mount Baker Ski Area. This race has drawn every big name in the sport, including Terje Haakonsen, Karleen Jeffery, Craig Kelly, Tom Sims, Victoria Jealouse, Barrett Christy, and Ross Rebagliati, snowboarding's first Olympic gold-medal winner. Along with stories in countless snow-related magazines, the race has been featured in mainstream publications such as *Outside* and *Sports Illustrated*. Not bad for a remote little ski area at the end of a dark, winding 57-mile road that doesn't lead anywhere.

But it's not just snowboarders at the Mount Baker Ski Area. Skiers love the terrain, too, and in fact still make up more than half of all rider visits.

Another of the Mount Baker Ski Area's major appeals is management's decision to focus less on frills (i.e., shops and après-ski) and more on the area's sublime setting at the foot of Mount Shuksan. There's no advertising on ski towers or trail maps. No video games. No televisions or neon signs. And, if it weren't for the power they're forced to generate themselves, no electricity. There still are no pay phones at the area, and cell phone coverage is nil to spotty at best.

All that is not to say that you're out of luck if you're dying for a steaming bowl of chili or piping mug of hot chocolate after a day on the slopes, or if you left your gloves or helmet at home. Both the White Salmon Day Lodge and the Heather Meadows Day Lodge offer food service with extensive menus and retail shops with all the gear you could possibly need. And the ski area's rental and instruction programs cater to all snow enthusiasts, from telemark skiers to snowshoers to cross-country skiers to, of course, alpine skiers and snowboarders.

Facts and Figures

Vertical rise: 1,500 feet.
White Salmon Day Lodge elevation: 3,500 feet.
Heather Meadows Day Lodge elevation: 4,300 feet.
Top elevation: Top of Hemispheres Chair, 5,089 feet.
Skiable acres: 1,000.
Lifts: Four quads, two doubles, two rope tows.
Terrain: 31 percent expert, 45 percent intermediate, 24 percent beginner.
Lift tickets: $37.
Season: Generally mid- to late November through the end of April.
Information: (360) 734–6771 or www.mtbaker.us.

In addition, the Mount Baker Ski Area offers access to some of the most lusted-after backcountry terrain around. But because the risk of avalanche here is quite high—several deaths have occurred in recent years—the ski area has imposed strict guidelines for those heading out-of-bounds. Warning signs not only remind those going beyond the ropes of the high avalanche potential but also what's required to do so: a partner, avalanche beacons and the ability to use them, a shovel, and knowledge of terrain, route, avalanche conditions, and forecast.

Throughout the season, the ski area often offers weekend snow safety awareness classes. Call the Mount Baker Ski Area at (360) 734–6771 for more information.

To get to the Mount Baker Ski Area from Bellingham, go east on the Mount Baker Highway for about 52 miles to the White Salmon Day Lodge. The Heather Meadows Day Lodge and parking areas are about 3 miles farther up the highway.

Heather Meadows

A whole world of snow possibilities exists and thrives just outside the boundaries of the Mount Baker Ski Area. The Picture and Highwood Lakes bowls, which show up in the foreground of countless scenic photo calendars that feature images of Mount Shuksan, fill with snow and become a magnet for folks with toboggans, sleds, giant tractor-trailer-tire tubes, plastic garbage bags, and just about anything people can come up with to slide downhill in the snow. (River kayaks seem to be popular as well.) Because you're not on ski area grounds, it's free, but of course you're not getting anything back in return. In other words, this ain't no snow-tube park, and it's up to you to hump back up the hill after catching a free ride from gravity down it. But that's half the fun anyway, isn't it?

An added bonus for playing here is that it's close to the Heather Meadows Day Lodge; thus hot cocoa and a place to warm those fingers and toes are never far away.

To get here, go east on the Mount Baker Highway to just past milepost 54 and Picture Lake. Start looking for parking here on the shoulder of the road that circles the lake, or park in the day lodge parking lot.

Backcountry Excursions

What follows are some basic route descriptions for various backcountry excursions. Because conditions vary so widely, and with winter travel there is no single trail to follow, they're thumbnail sketches. For current conditions and route descriptions, contact the Mount Baker Ranger District at (360) 856–5700.

Backcountry skiers and snowshoers are not likely to take exactly the same route, but they're similar enough that they're included here together. Skiers and snowboarders need to be avalanche aware, stay off slopes that are likely to slide, and not ski beyond their abilities. Snowshoers need to do the same and also remember to please stay out of skier-set tracks.

Note: Before heading out on this or any backcountry excursion, reread the sidebar on avalanches. And be aware that in early December 2003, three people were buried by an avalanche (two were rescued; one died) while they were snowshoeing to Artist Point. Major contributing factors: (1) It was snowing very heavily, and in fact, more than 2 feet of heavy, wet snow had fallen in the previous twenty-four hours; and (2) because visibility was so low, the snowshoers thought that rather than follow the ridge, they'd follow the path of the unplowed road. Unfortunately, they snowshoed on the lower parts of an unstable slope that slid and buried all three.

34 Upper Lodge to Artist Point

See map on pages 148–49.

TOTAL DISTANCE: Up to 4 miles round-trip.

TIME REQUIRED: 3 hours.

DIFFICULTY LEVEL: Moderate to difficult.

ELEVATION GAIN: 800 feet.

Permanent snowfield on Table Mountain

MAPS: Green Trails Mount Shuksan 14.

STARTING POINT: Heather Meadows Day Lodge parking lot.

THE TOUR: Drive east from Bellingham on the Mount Baker Highway for 55 miles to the Heather Meadows Day Lodge parking lot. (In winter and spring, that's as far as the road is plowed.) From the Heather Meadows Day Lodge parking lot (also known as the upper parking lot), the day trip to Artist Point— whether on skis or snowshoes—is one of the most spectacular winter adventures you'll experience. Accompanying you are huge, front-row views of Mount Shuksan, mantled in winter white, its icy glaciers an eerie blue. The giant anvil of snow-draped Table Mountain beckons you up to Artist Point, and when you make it there, you're greeted by truly awe-inspiring views of Mount Baker. The peace and serenity of this winter wonderland, along with the vista, make for a super experience.

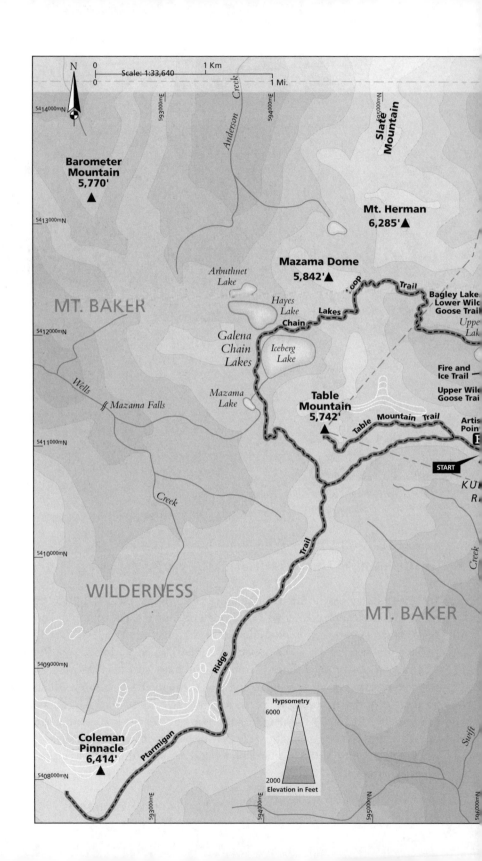

N

0   Scale: 1:33,640   1 Km
0   1 Mi.

5414000mN

593000mE

594000mE

595000mN

**Barometer
Mountain
5,770'**
▲

Slate
Mountain

5413000mN

Anderson Creek

**Mt. Herman
6,285'** ▲

**Mazama Dome
5,842'** ▲

Loop   Trail

**Bagley Lake
Lower Wild
Goose Trail**

*Arbuthnet
Lake*

MT. BAKER

*Hayes
Lake*   Lakes   Upper
Lake

5412000mN   Chain

*Galena
Chain
Lakes*   *Iceberg
Lake*

**Fire and
Ice Trail**

**Upper Wild
Goose Trail**

Wells   *ff Mazama Falls*   *Mazama
Lake*   **Table
Mountain
5,742'**   Table   Mountain   Trail   **Artist
Point**

5411000mN   ▲   P

START

Creek   **KU
R**

5410000mN   Trail

Creek

WILDERNESS   MT. BAKER

5409000mN   Ridge

Swift

**Coleman
Pinnacle
6,414'**   *Ptarmigan*

Hypsometry
6000

5408000mN   ▲   2000
Elevation in Feet

593000mE   594000mN   595000mN   59q000mN

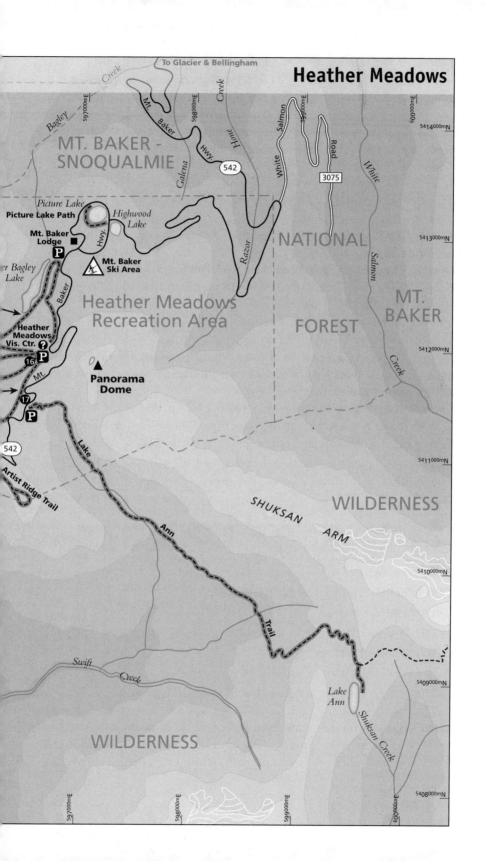

The way to Artist Point heads south, first along the unplowed road just west of the downhill skiers cruising the ski area's westernmost run. Past the last run, climb up toward Austin Pass, leaving the road, then regaining it, then leaving it, and so on. In general it's best to follow the obvious ridge and high meadows to Artist Point at the base of Table Mountain instead of the road, which switchbacks numerous times. It's not only shorter but also safer. You do regain the road, however, for the final 100 yards or so to Artist Point. Soak in the views, break out the hot cocoa, have a snowball fight. You'll think you're in heaven.

If conditions seem safe—not particularly warm, no new snow, not raining, etc.—and the snow seems unlikely to slide, a nice addition is to hike out Kulshan Ridge, the ridge leading southeast from Artist Point, in the direction of Mount Shuksan.

Options: Toward spring and early summer, as snowfall decreases, the snowpack consolidates, and avalanche potential drops, it's possible to add some farther destinations for some truly epic adventures.

Ptarmigan Ridge: From Artist Point, head along the south-facing flank of Table Mountain (see Hike 19 for a detailed Ptarmigan Ridge hiking trail description) for about a mile to the obvious ridge (Ptarmigan Ridge) that heads southwest toward Mount Baker and Coleman Pinnacle, a distinct shark fin of rock. Turn around and return the same way.

Chain Lakes: Follow the preceding description for Ptarmigan Ridge, but instead of heading southwest along the ridge toward Mount Baker, go right and drop down into the magical land of the iced-over Chain Lakes—Mazama, Iceberg, Hayes, and company (see Hike 16 for the Chain Lakes Loop hiking trail description).

35 Herman Saddle

See map on pages 148–49.

TOTAL DISTANCE: Up to 5 miles round-trip.

TIME REQUIRED: 4 hours.

DIFFICULTY LEVEL: Moderate to difficult.

ELEVATION GAIN: 1,000 feet.

MAPS: Green Trails Mount Shuksan 14.

STARTING POINT: Heather Meadows Day Lodge parking lot.

THE TOUR: Because this route requires dropping into at least one lake basin and contours along the steep south face of Mount Herman, this ski-snowshoe tour should be done only when avalanche potential is low. From the Heather Meadows Day Lodge parking lot, head south in the direction of Table Mountain. Where the slope angle and snow level seem conducive, drop into the Bagley Lakes basin and head to the right (west) in the direction of Herman Saddle, the obvious notch between Table Mountain and Mount Herman. That's your destination. From here it's all uphill, about 1,000 feet worth, to the saddle, about 2.5 miles from the parking lot.

Depending on conditions, your fitness level, and your desire, it's possible to continue on, dropping down into the Chain Lakes area (see the Options section in Hike 34). Keep in mind you'll be approaching the lakes from the opposite direction.

Nooksack Nordic Ski Club

This Bellingham-based club maintains three areas for cross-country skiing just off the Mount Baker Highway. When conditions allow, they brush, groom, and set tracks (including a lane for skate skiing) at the Salmon Ridge Sno-Park about 6 road miles below the Mount Baker Ski Area near the Silver Fir Campground. Because the elevation here is about 2,000 feet—or 1,500 to 3,000 feet lower than the ski area—snow levels can be iffy. It's best to check the Nooksack Nordic Ski Club Web site (www.nooksacknordicskiclub.org) or call the Glacier Public Service Center ranger (360–599–2714) for the latest conditions before heading to Salmon Ridge.

Skiing and snowshoeing are free at Salmon Ridge, though a Washington State nonmotorized Sno-Park Permit is required to park in the Salmon Ridge parking lot. Daily permits cost $8.00; season permits are $21.00; and they're available at local outdoor stores or by mail from the Washington State Winter Recreation Program (P.O. Box 42650, Olympia, WA 98504). Proceeds from permit sales go toward plowing parking lots and grooming trails.

Note to snowshoers: Stay out of set tracks lest you risk the wrath of dual-planked folks who might very well—and justifiably so—whack you with their ski poles and then schuss away in a flash. It's best to walk on the outside of set tracks, not between them, which is reserved for skate skiers.

The following are locations maintained by the Nooksack Nordic Ski Club.

Salmon Ridge (Razor Hone Road): Numerous mostly easy to intermediate trails can be found on and along this snow-covered route (Forest Service Road 3070) that parallels the North Fork Nooksack River for about 3 miles. You'll find glades of snow-laden trees and open meadows with views to Goat Mountain and the Nooksack Ridge, as well as gurgling creeks and of course the mighty Nooksack dashing by from Mount Shuksan to Puget Sound.

To get to the Salmon Ridge Sno-Park (permit required), go east on the Mount Baker Highway to milepost 46 and turn left into the large, signed parking lot across the road from Silver Fir Campground.

White Salmon Day Lodge at the Mount Baker Ski Area

Anderson Creek Road (Forest Service Road 3071): More than 6 miles of snow-covered road and trail beckon just across the Mount Baker Highway by the Silver Fir Campground. Forest Service Road 3071 heads west along the Nooksack, gaining only minimal elevation for the first 2.5 miles. Things steepen from there, with avalanche potential also increasing. For tame family fun, head right for the loops through riverfront Silver Fir Campground.

To get here, park at the Salmon Ridge Sno-Park (permit required) or, if there's room, near the Silver Fir Campground entrance.

White Salmon Road (Forest Service Road 3075): Located at an elevation of 3,400 feet, just about 1 road mile below the Mount Baker Ski Area White Salmon Day Lodge (lower lodge), White Salmon Road is the best bet for snow. In fact, most years, it's a given that the more than 2-mile-long White Salmon Road (as FR 3075 is also called) will be snow covered from November through April.

The road contours gently along the hillside, so the terrain is mostly easy and intermediate. And because the road travels through an old clear-cut, after the road turns the corner at about the 1-mile mark, the views are out of this world—rivaling almost any in the area. Glacier-clad Mount Shuksan is the main player, but also prominent are the Alaska-esque Nooksack Ridge, Goat and Ruth Mountains, and other peaks too numerous to mention. After the road rounds the bend and begins heading south (i.e., when the views become awesome), it descends gradually, eventually switchbacking into the White Salmon Creek Valley.

To get here, head east on the Mount Baker Highway to about milepost 51. The entrance is on the outside of a hairpin turn, but crossing the highway here can be dangerous. It's best to continue for about another mile to the White Salmon Day Lodge, turn around, and approach White Salmon Road that way. Parking is very limited.

Forest Service Roads

When the snow level allows, several of the Forest Service roads that are mentioned in this book as offering access to hiking trails during the summer and fall are used as backcountry ski and snowshoe routes. Be aware, however, that except for those mentioned in the Salmon Ridge Sno-Park section, these routes are not marked or maintained. Users proceed at their own risk and again are encouraged to call the Mount Baker Ranger District (360–856–5700) for the latest conditions before heading out. A Northwest Forest Pass is required for parking near trailheads on Forest Service roads.

Hannegan Pass Road: Located across the Nooksack River from the Salmon Ridge Sno-Park, this road offers some excellent snowshoeing and cross-country skiing in a magical mountain-and-river setting. Winter views of Mount Shuksan are huge, as are those of the river that pours from its Price Glacier and Price Lake, the North Fork of the Nooksack.

To get here, go east on the Mount Baker Highway to milepost 46.6 and turn left onto Hannegan Pass Road. As with the Salmon Ridge Sno-Park, snow is not a given here. Assuming the road is snow-covered, park in the obvious parking lot, and after strapping on the 'shoes or skis, head east along the road. After about 1.2 miles, the road forks. Go right and follow the sometimes overgrown road for about a mile to Ruth Creek. This makes a good lunch-hot cocoa-contemplate-life-while-you-stare-into-the-sparkling-waters-of-a-gurgling-creek turnaround point.

Wells Creek Road (Forest Service Road 33): This short jaunt to spectacular Nooksack Falls might not give you the workout you're looking for, but if you're a waterfall buff, it's one that will surely quench your thirst. Like the Salmon Ridge Sno-Park, snow is not always a sure thing here.

Nooksack Falls

Drive east on the Mount Baker Highway to milepost 40.5, and turn right onto Wells Creek Road (FR 33). Park on the side of the road or where the snow dictates. The road descends gently through quiet forest for about a half mile to a bridge overlooking the roaring, gushing Nooksack River as it plunges 170 feet to the rocky boulders below. Lower Wells Creek Falls, just to the south, add to the show as well. Stay behind all safety fences. Too many people, over the years, have maneuvered around the fence to get a better look, only to slip and fall to their deaths.

Depending on conditions and snow level, continue past the falls on Wells Creek Road for as far as conditions and your skill level allow. *Note:* As of press time, because of major flooding that occurred in October 2003, Wells Creek Road was washed out at about the 4-mile mark and had not yet been repaired. Call the ranger (360–599–2714 or 360–856–5700) for the latest conditions.

Twin Lakes Road (Forest Service Road 3065): This forested road begins climbing almost immediately from the Mount Baker Highway but eventually leads to open meadows with spectacular views of Mount Shuksan, Goat Mountain, and the Nooksack Ridge. To get here, drive east on the Mount Baker Highway to milepost 46.3. Park wherever space and the snow level allow. Open meadows are reached about 1.5 miles from the road's intersection with the Mount Baker Highway. After about 2 miles the road enters a narrow canyon where avalanche hazards increase dramatically; it's best to turn around here.

Glacier Creek Road (Forest Service Road 39): A couple of excellent tours offering stunning Mount Baker views can be found off this road, which heads due south (and up) toward Mount Baker from just outside Glacier. Because the road is not plowed, the starting point for this ski tour or snowshoe hike varies, as do distance and elevation gain. The lower the snow level, the longer the trip and higher the elevation gain, and vice versa.

To get here, drive east on the Mount Baker Highway to milepost 34.4 and turn right onto Glacier Creek Road (FR 39). Drive as far as the snow level allows. Because this road is groomed for snowmobiles, a Sno-Park Permit is required. When you can drive no farther, park and haul out the skis or 'shoes. (Be aware that snowmobilers also use this trail; thus your wintertime "Serenity Now" moments might be broken from time to time.) Follow the forested Forest Service road, admiring occasional glimpses down into Glacier Creek and up to Mount Baker. Pretend you're Edmund Coleman, who in 1868 became the first person to summit Mount Baker using much the same route as you're using now.

For Coal Pass: About a quarter mile before the summertime trailhead for the Heliotrope Ridge Trail (see Hike 9), go right at a fork onto Forest Service Road 36. This road continues to climb for another 2-plus miles to Coal Pass, a relative flat spot between the twin summits of Lookout Mountain.

For Mount Baker Viewpoint: Continue past the Heliotrope Trailhead, bearing to the right at a couple 90-plus degree turns, for a little more than a mile to an opening boasting perhaps the best Mount Baker vista to be found anywhere. The Coleman and Roosevelt Glaciers appear so close, you'll reach for your ice ax.

For Heliotrope Ridge and Coleman Glacier: As best you can, follow the summertime Heliotrope Ridge Trail (see Hike 9) to an up close and personal wintertime audience with this geologic wonder pouring ever so slowly from Mount Baker's northwest flank. Because of the route-finding skills required in trying to follow a forested, snow-covered trail, this is an experts-only route.

Canyon Creek Road (Forest Service Road 31): This road is a haven for snowmobilers so, while human-powered backcountry users (i.e., snowshoers and cross-country skiers) are welcome, they shouldn't expect the most serene of experiences. Weekdays, however, are more tame. Again, because the road is not plowed, the starting point varies for skiing or snowshoeing here, as do distance and elevation gain. The lower the snow level, the longer the trip and higher the elevation gain, and vice versa.

To get here, drive east on the Mount Baker Highway to milepost 35.3 and turn left onto Canyon Creek Road (FR 31). Drive as far as the snow level allows. The road climbs gradually up the North Fork Nooksack River valley, mostly in forest, with views down to Canyon Creek. About 7 miles up the road, a parking area is plowed on the right side of the road. Because this road is groomed for snowmobiles, a Sno-Park Permit is required. As the road contours around the north side of Church Mountain, views open up to reveal surrounding peaks.

Winter Hiking

If you're not much for snow or not the type interested in strapping contraptions to the bottoms of your feet in order to be mobile, several low-elevation hikes beckon you outdoors. Not especially long, these three trails are more walks than hikes but are more than worthwhile experiences any time of the year. Each is forested, and when the rain falls and the fog hangs heavy in the North Cascades, a wooded trail is one of the best places to be. And since these hikes are short with little elevation gain, they're a perfect excuse to get the whole family out of the house.

Boyd Creek Interpretive Trail: A short walk, mostly on boardwalk with interpretive signage about the lifestyles of local salmon. Go east on the Mount Baker Highway to milepost 34.3. Turn right onto Glacier Creek Road and then make a quick left onto Forest Service Road 37. The trailhead is 3.3 miles ahead on the right. (See Hike 1 for a complete trail description.)

Horseshoe Bend: The 1.2-mile (each way) trail snakes along the rushing Nooksack River. To get here, go east on the Mount Baker Highway to milepost

35.4, about 2 miles east of Glacier. The pullout parking lot is on the right. (See Hike 2 for a complete trail description.)

North Fork Nooksack Research Natural Area: Step way back in time and way deep into the woods on this half-mile path through trees some 700 years old. Go east on the Mount Baker Highway to about milepost 43.9. The roadside pullout parking area is easy to miss, so slow down well before. (See Hike 3 for a complete trail description.)

Eagle Viewing

Each year from November through February, about 200 eagles converge on a stretch of the Nooksack River near Deming to dine on salmon. Though about 17 miles west of the area covered in this book, this eagle-viewing site is included because it's easy to get to—in fact, it's on the way to much of the area that this book covers—and is one heck of a show.

Along with soaring slowly overhead, the eagles can be seen perched rather regally in trees and feeding on spawning and dying chum salmon along the river's banks and gravel bars. Visitors are urged not to approach or otherwise disturb the eagles, even if they're incredibly close and seem oblivious to you (which they often are). Eagles need to conserve their energy as much as possible, and they waste it if they have to flee humans trying to get too close.

The best hours to see them on the ground are between sunrise and about 11:00 A.M. And don't be discouraged if it's cloudy or overcast; those are actually the best days for eagle viewing because the birds are more apt to conserve their energy and hang out in the trees along the river. On sunny days, they're more apt to take to the skies and be harder to spot.

Two of the best places to spot the eagles follow.

Mosquito Lake Road: Head east on the Mount Baker Highway to just before milepost 17 and Mosquito Lake Road. Turn right and follow the road for about three-quarters of a mile to a bridge over the Nooksack River. Park just ahead on the side of the road. Watch from the bridge.

Another pullout spot can be found a mile down North Fork Road, which can be accessed by taking a left about a quarter mile past the Nooksack River bridge.

Very important: When parking at either of these spots, be sure to respect private property, and don't park at the nearby fire station.

Deming Homestead Eagle Park: Go east from Bellingham on the Mount Baker Highway for 15 miles to Truck Road. The turnoff is just past the Highway 9 intersection in Deming. Turn right onto Truck Road and follow it for a half mile. The well-signed park is on your right. This Whatcom County park has about one-third mile of riverfront access, with about the same distance of level, easy walking path. There are picnic tables, interpretive signs, and a covered observation shelter for eagle spotting on inclement days.

South Side

While the Baker Lake basin doesn't boast its own ski area the way the north side has the Mount Baker Ski Area, there's still plenty of winter snow fun to be had on the south side of the big mountains. At its highest point Baker Lake Road climbs to only about 1,100 feet and can be snow-free year-round, so visitors usually need to drive one of the many Forest Service roads to reach the snow.

For those who aren't snow enthusiasts, however, Baker Lake Road's relatively low elevation is a plus—trails such as Baker River and Baker Lake can be hikable year-round. And those with a bent for bald eagles are in luck. Just east of the Baker Lake basin, a 10-mile stretch of the Skagit River plays host to one of the largest concentrations of wintering bald eagles in the Lower 48 states.

Backcountry Excursions

Shadow of the Sentinels Sno-Park

When the snow level is low enough, the Shadow of the Sentinels parking lot (see Hike 20) is plowed free of snow, and a Sno-Park Permit is required to park here. However, since this trail's elevation is only about 1,000 feet above sea level, it's not uncommon for it to remain snow-free all year.

Forest Service Roads

As on the north side, in winter and spring several Forest Service roads that lead to popular hiking trails become destinations themselves for snowshoers and cross-country skiers. Again, these routes are not marked or maintained for skiers or snowshoers. Because some of these roads are Snowmobile Sno-Parks (that is, groomed for snowmobile use), expect lots of motorized snow enthusiasts, especially on weekends. But skiers and snowshoers are welcome, too, and as long as all users respect one another—that is, stay out of each other's tracks—everyone can enjoy this winter wonderland.

Call the Mount Baker Ranger District (360–856–5700) for the latest conditions before heading out. On most of the following roads, a Sno-Park Permit is required. A Northwest Forest Pass is required for parking near trailheads on Forest Service roads.

Forest Service Roads 12 and 13: Depending on the snow level, these snow-covered roads to the popular Schreibers Meadow hiking area provide a number of superb winter-spring snow experiences. Later in spring, as the snow level rises, it's possible to ski or snowshoe the lower reaches of some of the trails from the meadows and be rewarded with megahuge views of Mount Baker. As

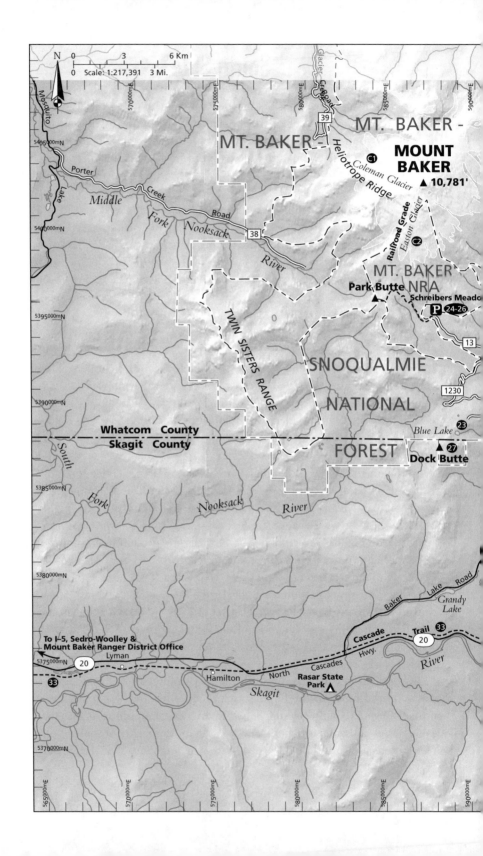

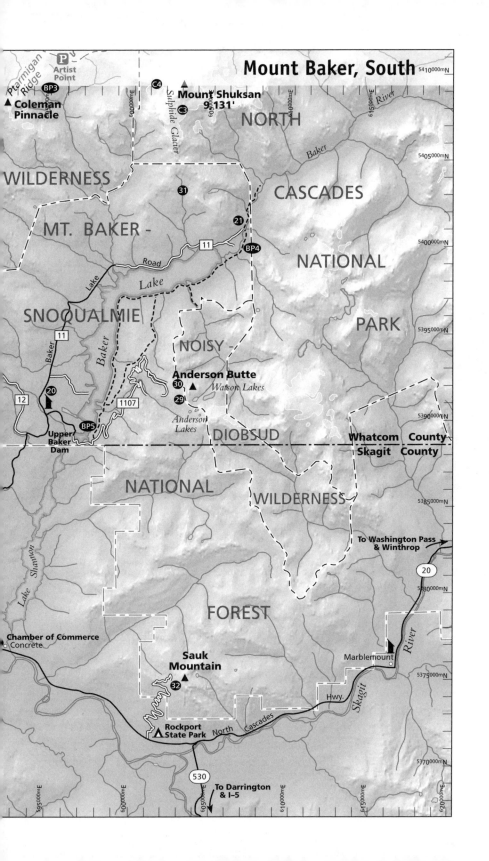

Ptarmigan Ridge

BP3

P Artist Point

▲ **Coleman Pinnacle**

C4

▲ **Mount Shuksan 9,131'**

C3 Sulphide Glacier

NORTH

Baker River

WILDERNESS

CASCADES

MT. BAKER -

31

21

11

Road

BP4

Lake

Lake

NATIONAL

SNOQUALMIE

11

Baker

Baker

20

12

1107

BP5

NOISY -

Anderson Butte

30 ▲ Watson Lakes

29

Anderson Lakes

Upper Baker Dam

DIOBSUD

PARK

5410000mN

5405000mN

5400000mN

5395000mN

5390000mN

Whatcom County
Skagit County

NATIONAL

WILDERNESS

5385000mN

To Washington Pass & Winthrop

20

5380000mN

Chamber of Commerce Concrete

FOREST

Sauk Mountain

▲

Lake Shannon

Marblemount

Skagit River

5375000mN

32

Hwy.

Rockport ▲ **State Park**

North Cascades

530

To Darrington & I-5

5370000mN

Springtime view of Mount Shuksan

with all of these routes, distance and elevation gain vary depending on the snow level and thus where each route begins.

To get here, go east on Highway 20 to just past milepost 82. Turn left onto Baker Lake Road and, in 12.2 miles, left onto FR 12. If the snow level is especially low, park here (Sno-Park Permit required) and follow the forested road for up to 12 miles (one way) depending on your fitness level, inclination, and skill level. More than likely, however, FR 12 will be drivable for another 3 miles to the intersection with FR 13, where you can park.

After stepping into your skis or snowshoes, here are your choices: Head right up FR 13 for about 6 miles (one way) toward the Schreibers Meadow parking lot. Or, for a little less snowmobile presence, continue straight, remaining on FR 12 for another 3.8 miles to Forest Service Road 1230. The road then continues for about 4 more miles, finally ending at the Blue Lake and Dock Butte Trailhead. (See Hikes 23 and 27 for complete trail descriptions.)

Forest Service Road 1107 (Anderson Creek Road): Not to be confused with the Anderson Creek Road on the north side of Mount Baker in the Salmon Ridge Sno-Park, this road leads from the south end of Baker Lake to the popular summertime Anderson-Watson Lakes hiking area. The road climbs high above Baker Lake's east shore, breaking out of the trees and offering panoramic views of both Mounts Baker and Shuksan. The road starts low—about 725 feet above sea level—and you'll likely be able to drive several miles of road (getting you closer to the views) before putting on the skis or snowshoes.

To get here, go east on Highway 20 to just past milepost 82. Turn left onto Baker Lake Road. At milepost 13.8, turn right onto gravel Forest Service Road 1106 (Baker Lake Dam Road). Cross Baker Dam in about 1.5 miles, and in 0.6 mile past that, turn left onto FR 1107. From the dam to the Anderson-Watson Lakes Trailhead, it's just over 10 miles, but you'll be able to drive a lot of that. When you can drive no farther, park in the Sno-Park lot. (A Sno-Park Permit is required.)

Kulshan Campground

When the snow level is unusually low—about 500 feet or less—this Puget Sound Energy campground, just a half mile from Baker Lake Dam, boasts some interesting cross-country skiing and snowshoeing possibilities. Head north from the campground, cross a bridge, and schuss your way along a lakeside road with spectacular views of not only the lake but also surrounding peaks including Mounts Shuksan and Blum. A short climb to the right before the bridge leads to an interesting viewpoint.

To get here, go east on Highway 20 to just past milepost 82. Turn left onto Baker Lake Road. At milepost 13.8, turn right onto gravel Forest Service Road 1106 (Baker Lake Dam Road) and follow it for 1.3 miles to Kulshan Campground on the left.

Baker Lake Road

Again, if the snow is really low, it's possible to cross-country ski and snowshoe the last 6 unpaved miles of Baker Lake Road all the way to the Baker River Trailhead. Much of this stretch follows the lake's shoreline and as such provides winter water and mountain views that are out of this world. Be aware that because this isn't a Sno-Park, SUVs and other four-wheel-drive vehicles are allowed on the road.

To get here, go east on Highway 20 to just past milepost 82, about 15 miles past Sedro-Woolley. Turn left onto Baker Lake Road and continue north to milepost 20.4 where the pavement ends.

Trail of Two Rivers

Just east of the area covered in this book, a Forest Service road to a popular summer trail—Forest Service Road 1030 (Sauk Mountain Road)—rewards hikers and skiers with views down to a meeting of two great rivers—the Skagit and the Sauk—and more than a few great mountains. But they have to work for it, earn their turns as it were. The road is steep, and the multiple switchbacks can seem endless.

To get here, go east on Highway 20 to milepost 96, about 7 miles east of Concrete, 29 miles east of Sedro-Woolley. Turn left onto Sauk Mountain Road (FSR 1030), just before Rockport State Park. Drive as far as the snow level allows. The road is just less than 8 miles to the trailhead and, depending on the snow level, you should be able to drive a couple of those miles. Then get out the gear, strap it on, and go.

Climb through forest and clear-cut meadows, switchbacking relentlessly until the first south-facing valley and mountain views show up about 5 miles from Highway 20. Views improve the higher you go and the closer you get to the summer trailhead. But because the road crosses a number of avalanche chutes, so does the chance of snowslide. Proceed at your own risk. And because the summer trail itself switches back and forth across a steep, avalanche-prone slope, it's best to leave it to summer.

Winter Hiking

An advantage of many of the trails in the Baker Lake basin being at a low elevation is that they're often passable year-round, if a little muddily. And while each of the following hikes or walks is family-friendly (i.e., they don't gain a lot of elevation), for those who like a little distance in their winter walking, the Baker Lake Trail offers up to 14 miles' worth (one way). There are even a few places along the trail to pitch the tent for some winter camping.

Here are a few that make for great winter adventures.

Baker Lake Trail (South Entrance): Stately old-growth trees (that somehow seem even more stately and old when shrouded in winter's mists and fog) provide peekaboo lake and mountain views and not much elevation gain. The trail is 14-plus miles long (one way), but numerous points along the trail make for fitting turnaround spots. Anderson Point Camp, about 2 miles from the trailhead, is a good one.

To get here, go east on Highway 20 to just past milepost 82. Turn left onto Baker Lake Road and follow it for 13.8 miles to Baker Lake Dam Road (Forest Service Road 1106). Continue for about 3 miles—along the way, the road crosses the top of the Baker Lake Dam and becomes Forest Service Road 1107—to the trailhead parking lot, which is on the left. (See Hike 22 for a complete trail description.)

Shadow of the Sentinels: Five-hundred-plus-year-old trees are the highlight of this half-mile, barrier-free boardwalk walk. It seems most fitting to visit this small-scale rain forest in winter and spring when the weather is wettest. Go east on Highway 20 to just past milepost 82. Turn left onto Baker Lake Road. Continue for 15 miles. The trailhead parking lot is on the right. In winter and early spring a Sno-Park Permit is required. (See Hike 20 for a complete trail description.)

Baker River Trail and Baker Lake Trail (North Entrance): Both of the trails near the north end of Baker Lake give you the true wintertime alpine river experience. The Baker River, which feeds Baker Lake, can be anything from a mellow gurgle to a raging torrent to a snowy winter wonderland featuring frozen pools of ice. Go east on Highway 20 to just past milepost 82. Turn left onto Baker Lake Road and follow it for 26 miles to the end. The Baker River and Baker Lake hikes share the same trailhead and trail for the first half mile. The Baker Lake Trail then heads east over the Baker River and continues for 14 miles (one way). (See Hikes 21 and 28 for complete trail descriptions.)

Rockport State Park, just east of the Baker Lake basin, boasts 5 miles of walking and hiking trails, much of it through a 600-acre stand of forest that's never been logged. Massive old growth never seems more primeval and otherworldly than in winter and spring's rain and fog. To get here, head east on Highway 20 to milepost 96.5, about 14 miles east of Baker Lake Road and 7 miles east of Concrete. The well-signed park is on the left (north).

Canoeing and Kayaking

Because winter and spring are generally mild down low in the Baker Lake basin, canoeing or kayaking the big lake during the colder weather months can be a terrific experience. A peaceful one, too. The campgrounds aren't open yet, but ski slopes are in full swing, so the crowds are off doing other things. (The frigid water probably scares off its fair share of potential paddlers as well.) But if you're a paddling enthusiast who's got the cold-weather gear and a love for views of massive mountains cloaked in winter white, then 9-mile-long Baker Lake makes for a super winter outing.

But watch out for them stumps. Baker Lake is a Puget Sound Energy reservoir, and its level fluctuates according to snowmelt, rain, and energy demand. This time of year, the water level is generally lower, revealing thousands of tree stumps from the days when Baker Lake was still forest. And with the lower level, you'll more than likely have to drag your boat for a bit through the mud before you put in. But what's a little mud when you can have such a big body of water pretty much to yourself? And remember: dress warmly.

Campgrounds with boat launches are good put-in spots, particularly Horseshoe Cove and Panorama Point. To get to Horseshoe Cove, drive north on

Baker Lake Road to milepost 15.2 and turn right. Follow signs for the campground. For Panorama Point, head north to milepost 19.3 and turn right.

Eagle Viewing

"Birds of a feather flock together" goes the old saying, and each winter along the Skagit River, hundreds of bald eagles do just that. Between Rockport and Marblemount, a 9-mile stretch of the Skagit just southeast of the Baker Lake basin plays host to between 400 and 600 eagles who make the river's banks and nearby forests their seasonal home. It's not unusual to see a few dozen eagles in a single tree, hung like Christmas ornaments for the holidays. They fly in from as far away as Alaska and Montana to feed on the Skagit's spawning and dying chum salmon. It's the largest annual gathering of eagles in the Lower 48 states.

Eagles begin arriving sometime in December and usually stay around through February. The numbers generally peak during the last week of December and the first week of January, just after the peak time for salmon spawning. After spending their days on the river, in late afternoons the eagles head for the hills, as it were, to roost—spending their evenings and nights in old-growth trees around Rockport State Park and near milepost 100.

The average eagle stands almost 3 feet tall, weighs nine pounds, and has a wingspan of 6 feet. Both males and females sport the characteristic white heads and tails, though they're not so adorned until they reach maturity at about three years. (Eagles live up to twenty years in the wild and sometimes forty in captivity.) Juveniles, of which there are many at this annual gathering, are a mottled-brown color and often are mistaken for golden eagles.

The best spots for eagle viewing are the following.

Highway 20 Milepost 100 Rest Area: This riverside pullout area has picnic benches, portable toilets, and interpretive eagle displays. On weekends during eagle season, it is staffed by volunteers who set up spotting scopes and provide eagle information. As the name implies, this area is located right at Highway 20 milepost 100, on the right.

Howard Miller Steelhead Park: On eagle season weekends, volunteers help you spot eagles at this riverside park. The park is located near the intersection of Highway 20 and Highway 530, just past Rockport State Park near Highway 20 milepost 98.

Skagit River Bald Eagle Interpretive Center: Open Friday through Sunday during eagle season, the center features guest speakers, slide presentations, a gift shop, and guided eagle walks through nearby Howard Miller Steelhead Park. The center is located on Alfred Street, just before the intersection of Highway 20 and Highway 530. For more information, check the Web site at www.skagiteagle.org.

Here are a few eagle-viewing tips.

- Do not approach or otherwise disturb the eagles, even if they're incredibly close and seem oblivious to you (which they often are). Eagles need to conserve their energy as much as possible, and they waste it if they have to flee humans attempting to get a better look.

- The best eagle-viewing hours are between sunrise and 11:00 A.M. Don't be discouraged if it's cloudy or overcast; those are actually the best days for seeing these stately birds, as they're more likely then to conserve their energy by hanging out in trees along the river. On sunny days, they're more apt to take to the skies and be harder to spot.

- Dress warmly for the weather. Bring along rain gear, too. If it's not raining now, that just means it's about to start.

If watching the eagles from land doesn't cut it for you—if, say, you'd like a salmon's-eye view—a number of rafting companies offer eagle float trips. These are not heart-stopping, rapid-hopping, boulder-bouncing, thrill-a-minute white-water adventures but rather tame floats wherein the object is to (1) spot as many eagles as you can while (2) disturbing them as little as possible. These trips usually last about three hours and, as they take place in the middle of winter on a river, can be quite chilly. So layer, layer, layer, and break out the Gore-Tex shell for on top.

Here are some guide services that run Skagit River eagle float trips.

- Pacific NW Float Trips, (866) 298–6287, www.pacificnwfloattrips.com
- Alpine Adventures, (800) 723–8386, www.alpineadventures.com
- River Recreation, (800) 464–5899, www.riverrecreation.com
- River Riders, (800) 448–7238, www.riverrider.com

Dining and Lodging

There are numerous dining and lodging opportunities in the Mount Baker–Mount Shuksan area that don't involve sleeping bags or camp stoves. The small towns of Glacier and Maple Falls on the north side and Concrete and Sedro-Woolley on the south side offer restaurants, motels, B&Bs, condos, and other lodgings. Here are a few.

North Side

Places to Eat

Graham's at Mount Baker, 9989 Mount Baker Highway, Glacier; (360) 599–1964 or www.grahams restaurant.com

Maple Fuels Wash-A-Ton, 7797 Silver Lake Road (Mount Baker MP 25.8), Maple Falls; (360) 599–2222

Milano's Market & Deli, 9990 Mount Baker Highway, Glacier; (360) 599–2863

Places to Stay

Glacier Creek Lodge, 10036 Mount Baker Highway, Glacier; (800) 719–1414 or www.glacier creeklodge.com

The Inn at Mount Baker, P.O. Box 5150, Glacier, 98244; (360) 599–1776 or www.theinnatmt baker.com

Mount Baker Lodging, rents various cabins, cottages, and condos in Glacier and Maple Falls; (800) 709–7669 or www.mtbaker lodging.com

Snowline Inn, 10433 Mount Baker Highway, Glacier; (800) 228–0119 or www.snowlineinn.com

For more information on eateries and lodgings, check the Mount Baker Foothills Chamber of Commerce Web site at www.mtbakerchamber .org or call (360) 599–1518.

South Side

Places to Eat

Annie's Pizza Station, 44568 Highway 20, Concrete; (360) 853–7227

Buzz Inn Steak House, 1975 Highway 20, Sedro-Woolley; (360) 854–9365

Iron Skillet, 132 West State Street, Sedro-Woolley; (360) 855–0080

North Cascades Inn, 44618 Highway 20, Concrete; (800) 251–3054 or www.north-cascade-inn.com

Places to Stay

Cascade Mountain Inn, 40418 Pioneer Lane, Concrete; (888) 652–8127 or www.cascade-mtn -inn.com

North Cascade Inn, 44618 Highway 20, Concrete; (800) 251–3054 or www.north-cascade-inn.com

Ovenell's Heritage Inn, 46276 Concrete-Sauk Valley Road, Concrete; (866) 464–3414 or www.ovenells-inn.com

Skagit Motel, 1977 Highway 20, Sedro-Woolley; (800) 582–9121

Three Rivers Inn, 210 Ball Street, Sedro-Woolley; (800) 221–5122

For more information on places to eat or spend the night, check the Concrete Chamber of Commerce at www.concrete-wa.com (360–853–7042) or the Sedro-Woolley chamber at www.sedro-woolley.com (360–855–1841).

Annual Events

January

Legendary Banked Slalom snow-board race, Mount Baker Ski Area; (360) 734–6771 or www.mtbakerski area.com

February

Skagit Bald Eagle Festival, Concrete, Rockport, and Marblemount; (360) 853–7283 or www.skagiteagle .org

May

Ski to Sea relay race, Mount Baker Ski Area to Bellingham; (360) 734–1330 or www.skitosea.com/ skitosea

July

Loggerodeo Fourth of July celebration, Sedro-Woolley; (800) 214–0800 or www.loggerodeo.com

Mount Baker Blues Festival, Deming; (360) 671–6817 or www.bakerblues.com

September

Mount Baker Hill Climb bike race, Glacier to Artist Point; www.meyermemorial.org

October

Baker Lake 50K Trail Run, Baker Lake; (360) 387–4688 or www.baker lake50k.com

For More Information

Mount Baker–Snoqualmie National
  Forest
Mount Baker Ranger District
810 State Route 20
Sedro-Woolley, WA 98284
(360) 856–5700
www.fs.fed.us/r6/mbs
Note: North Cascades National Park
offices are in the same building and
are reached via the same phone number. The park Web site is
www.nps.gov/noca.

Mount Baker Ranger District
Glacier Public Service Center
10091 Mount Baker Highway
Concrete, WA 98244
(360) 599–2714

Washington Department of Fish
  and Wildlife
North Puget Sound Region
16018 Mill Creek Boulevard
Mill Creek, WA 98012
(425) 775–1311
www.wdfw.wa.gov

Rockport State Park
(360) 853–8461
www.parks.wa.gov; click on Park
  Information

Rasar State Park
(360) 826–3942
www.parks.wa.gov; click on Park
  Information

Silver Lake Park
(360) 599–2776
www.co.whatcom.wa.us/parks/silver
  lake/silverlake.jsp

National Recreation Reservation
  Service
(to reserve campsites at national
  forest campgrounds)
(877) 444–6777
www.reserveusa.com

Baker Lake Resort
(888) 711–3033

Kulshan Campground
(888) 711–3033

North Cascades Institute
(360) 856–5700
www.ncascades.org

Mount Baker Ski Area (business
  address)
1019 Iowa Street
Bellingham, WA 98229
(360) 734–6771
Snow report: (360) 671–0211 or
  (206) 634–0200
www.mtbaker.us

Nooksack Nordic Ski Club
(360) 671–4502
www.nooksacknordicskiclub.org

Northwest Weather and Avalanche
   Center
(206) 526–6677
www.nwac.noaa.gov

Mount Baker Hiking Club
(360) 332–3195
www.mountbakerclub.org

Bellingham Mountaineers
(360) 403–4810
www.bellinghammountaineers.org

Skagit Alpine Club
(360) 853–8901
www.skagitalpineclub.com

Concrete Chamber of Commerce
(360) 853–7042
www.concrete-wa.com

Sedro-Woolley Chamber of
   Commerce
(360) 855–1841
www.sedro-woolley.com

Mount Baker Foothills Chamber
   of Commerce
(360) 599–1518
www.mtbakerchamber.org

Bellingham/Whatcom County
   Convention and Visitors Bureau
(360) 671–3990
www.bellingham.org

Mount Vernon Chamber of
   Commerce
(360) 428–8547
www.mountvernonchamber.com

Burlington Chamber of Commerce
(360) 757–0994
www.burlington-chamber.com

Marblemount
(800) 875–2448
www.marblemount.com

Index

A

accommodations, 169–70
Anderson Butte hike, 114
Anderson Creek Road, 152
Anderson–Watson Lakes Trail hike,
    111, 113, 130
Annie's Pizza Station, 169
annual events, 171
Artist Point, 71
Artist Point, Upper Lodge to,
    backcountry snow excursion,
    146–47, 150
Artist Ridge Trail hike, 36–37
Austin Pass Picnic Area, 23, 71
avalanches, 142–43

B

backcountry camping, 74–75
backcountry snow excursions,
    146–47, 150–53, 155–56, 159,
    162–64
backpacking trips, 75, 77–78, 131–32
Bagley Lakes–Lower Wild Goose
    Trail hike, 33, 35
Baker Lake, taking photographs
    of, 125
Baker Lake Dam, 123
Baker Lake 50K Trail Run, 171
Baker Lake Resort, 123, 127, 172
Baker Lake Road, 12, 13–14, 138, 163
Baker Lake Trail backpacking
    trip, 131
Baker Lake Trail–North Entrance
    hike, 110–11, 129
Baker Lake Trail–North Entrance
    winter hike, 165
Baker Lake Trail–South Entrance
    hike, 98–100, 129

Baker Lake Trail–South Entrance
    winter hike, 164
Baker River Trail hike, 95, 98, 131
Baker River Trail winter hike, 165
bald eagles, viewing/taking
    photographs of, 125, 128, 157
bears, encounters with, 8–9
Bellingham Mountaineers, 173
Bellingham/Whatcom County
    Convention and Visitors
    Bureau, 173
biking, 85–87, 137–38
black flies, 9–10
Blue Lake Trail hike, 100, 102, 131
Boulder Creek Campground, 126
Boyd Creek Interpretive Trail hike,
    25, 69
Boyd Creek Interpretive Trail
    winter hike, 156
Burlington Chamber of
    Commerce, 173
Buzz Inn Steak House, 169

C

camping
    backcountry, 74–75, 130–31
developed campgrounds, 73–74,
    125–29
hiker sites, 74, 129
canoeing and kayaking, 134, 136–37,
    165–66
Canyon Creek Road, 19, 156
Canyon Ridge Trail bike route, 87
Cascade Mountain Inn, 169
Cascade Trail bike route, 138
Cascade Trail hike, 119, 121
Chain Lakes Loop–Ptarmigan Ridge
    backpacking trip, 78

Chain Lakes Loop Trail hike, 57, 60–62, 74
chambers of commerce, 173
Chilliwack River Valley–Whatcom Pass–Copper Ridge backpacking trip, 75, 77
Church Mountain Trail hike, 44, 46, 75
climbing instruction, 84–85
climbs, 78, 80, 83, 132, 134
Coleman Pinnacle scramble, 84
Concrete Chamber of Commerce, 173
Copper Ridge–Chilliwack River Valley–Whatcom Pass backpacking trip, 75, 77
cougars, encounters with, 9
cross-country skiing, 146–47, 150–53, 155–56, 159, 162–64

D

Damfino Lakes–Excelsior Mountain–High Divide Trails hike, 46, 48–49, 75
Deming Homestead Eagle Park, 157
developed campgrounds, 73–74, 125–29
dining, 169–70
Dock Butte Trail hike, 109–10
dogs, 11
Douglas Fir Campground, 73
Douglas Fir Campground Picnic Site, 69
downhill skiing, 139, 142–45
driving tours, summer/fall
  north side, 15, 18–19, 21–23
  south side, 89, 92
  weather conditions for, 15

E

eagles, viewing/taking photographs of, 125, 128, 157, 166–67
etiquette, trail, 10–11

Excelsior Group Campground, 73
Excelsior Mountain–High Divide–Damfino Lakes Trails hike, 46, 48–49, 75

F

fall driving tours. *See* summer/fall driving tours
festivals, 171
Fire and Ice Trail hike, 35, 71
fishing, 137
forests (ancient), taking photographs of, 72, 125
Forest Service Road 31 (Canyon Creek Road) bike route, 87
Forest Service Road 32 (Hannegan Pass Road) bike route, 86
Forest Service Road 37 (Deadhorse Creek Road) bike route, 86
Forest Service Road 1106/Kulshan Campground bike route, 137
Forest Service Road 1107, 163
Forest Service Road 1107 bike route, 138
Forest Service Road 3070 (Razor Hone Road) bike route, 86
Forest Service Roads 12 and 13, 159, 162–63

G

geologic history, 2–3
Glacier Creek Lodge, 169
Glacier Creek Road, 155–56
Glacier Public Service Center, 18, 69, 172
glaciers, 3–4, 40–41, 125
Graham's at Mount Baker, 169

H

handicapped-accessible areas, 68–71, 123–24
Hannegan Pass Road, 153

Hannegan Pass Trail hike, 54, 56–57, 75
Hannegan Peak scramble, 84
Heather Meadows Area, 13, 145–46
Heather Meadows Visitor Center, 22, 71
Heliotrope Ridge Trail, 38, 40–41, 75
Herman Saddle backcountry snow excursion, 150–51
High Divide backpacking trip, 77
High Divide–Damfino Lakes–Excelsior Mountain Trails hike, 46, 48–49, 75
High Pass–Winchester Mountain Lookout Trails hike, 52, 54, 75
Highway 20 Milepost 100 Rest Area, 166
Horseshoe Bend Trail hike, 25, 27
Horseshoe Bend winter hike, 156–57
Horseshoe Cove Campground, 126
Horseshoe Cove Campground Picnic Area, 123
Howard Miller Steelhead Park, 166

I
Inn at Mount Baker, The, 169
insects, 9–10
Iron Skillet, 169

K
kayaking and canoeing, 134, 136–37, 165–66
Kulshan Campground, 123, 125–26, 163, 172

L
Lake Ann Trail hike, 62–63, 74
lakes, taking photographs of, 72, 125
Legendary Banked Slalom snowboard race, 143–44, 171
lodging, 169–70
Loggerodeo Fourth of July celebration, 171

Lower Wild Goose Trail–Bagley Lakes hike, 33, 35

M
Maple Fuels Wash-A-Ton, 169
Marblemount, 173
Milano's Market & Deli, 169
Mosquito Lake Road, 157
mountain biking, 85–87, 137–38
mountain-climbing instruction, 84–85
Mount Baker, taking photographs of, 71, 124
Mount Baker Blues Festival, 171
Mount Baker climb, 78, 80, 132, 134
Mount Baker Foothills Chamber of Commerce, 173
Mount Baker Highway (Scenic Byway), 11, 12–13
Mount Baker Hiking Club, 173
Mount Baker Hill Climb bike race, 171
Mount Baker Lodge, 6
Mount Baker Lodging, 169
Mount Baker Marathon, 7
Mount Baker National Recreation Area, 8
Mount Baker Ski Area, 139, 142–45, 172
Mount Baker–Snoqualmie National Forest, 172
Mount Baker Viewpoint Picnic Site, 69
Mount Baker Wilderness Area, 8
Mount Shuksan, taking photographs of, 71, 124
Mount Shuksan climb, 80, 134
Mount Vernon Chamber of Commerce, 173
movies, 6–7
Mt. Baker–Mount Shuksan area
accessing, 11–12
attempts to scale mountains, 4–5

differing appearance of mountains, 1–2
glaciers, 3–4
as a Hollywood movie site, 6–7
management of, 2
naming of mountains, 3
natural and cultural history of, 2–3
as a tourist destination, 5–8

N

National Recreation Reservation Service, 172
Nooksack Falls, 19
Nooksack Nordic Ski Club, 151, 172
North Cascade Inn, 169, 170
North Cascades Institute, 172
North Cascades National Park, 8
North Fork Nooksack Research Natural Area hike, 27, 29, 32
North Fork Nooksack Research Natural Area winter hike, 157
Northwest Forest Passes, 5
Northwest Weather and Avalanche Center, 173

O

Ovenell's Heritage Inn, 170

P

Panorama Point Campground, 126–27
Panorama Point Campground Picnic Area, 123
Park Butte–Scott Paul–Railroad Grade Trail backpacking trip, 132
Park Butte Trail hike, 104, 106, 131
Park Creek Campground, 127
photographs, best opportunities for, 71–72, 124–25
Picture Lake, 70–71
Picture Lake Path hike, 32

Ptarmigan Ridge–Chain Lakes Loop backpacking trip, 78
Ptarmigan Ridge Trail hike, 65, 67, 74
Puget Sound Energy Baker River Visitor Center, 124

R

Railroad Grade–Park Butte–Scott Paul Trails backpacking trip, 132
Railroad Grade Trail hike, 106–7, 131
Rasar State Park, 124, 129, 172
restaurants, 169–70
river rafting, 85
rivers, taking photographs of, 72, 125
road biking, 87, 138
rock-climbing instruction, 84–85
rock hounding, 63
Rockport State Park, 124, 128–29, 165, 172
Ruth Mountain climb, 80, 83

S

Salmon Ridge, 151
Sauk Mountain Trail hike, 117, 119, 131
Schreibers Meadow, 102, 104
Scott Paul–Railroad Grade–Park Butte Trails backpacking trip, 132
Scott Paul Trail hike, 107, 109, 131
scrambles, 83–84
"sea of peaks" effect, taking photographs of, 72
seasonal events, 171
Sedro-Woolley Chamber of Commerce, 173
Shadow of the Sentinels Sno-Park, 159
Shadow of the Sentinels Trail hike, 94–95, 123
Shadow of the Sentinels winter hike, 165

Shannon Creek Campground, 127–28

Shannon Creek Campground Picnic Area, 124

Shannon Ridge Trail hike, 115, 131

Shuksan Picnic Area, 69–70

Silver Fir Campground, 73

Silver Fir Campground Picnic Area, 70

Silver Lake Park, 74, 172

Skagit Alpine Club, 173

Skagit Bald Eagle Festival, 171

Skagit Motel, 170

Skagit River Bald Eagle Interpretive Center, 166

skiing
backcountry excursions, 146–47, 150–53, 155–56, 159, 162–64
downhill, 139, 142–45

Ski to Sea relay race, 7, 171

Skyline Divide Trail hike, 42, 44, 75

snow, 10

Snowline Inn, 169

snowshoeing, 146–47, 150–53, 155–56, 159, 162–64

summer/fall driving tours
north side, 15, 18–19, 21–23
south side, 89, 92
weather conditions for, 15

T

Table Mountain hike, 63–65, 74

ten essentials, 38

Three Rivers Inn, 170

Tomyhoi Lake–Yellow Aster Butte Trails hike, 49, 51, 75

Tomyhoi Peak scramble, 83–84

trail etiquette, 10–11

Trail of Two Rivers, 164

trees, 9, 72, 125

Twin Lakes Road, 155

U

Upper Lodge to Artist Point backcountry snow excursion, 146–47, 150

Upper Wild Goose Trail hike, 35–36

V

volcanoes, 2–3

W

Washington Department of Fish and Wildlife, 172

waterfalls, taking photographs of, 72

Watson–Anderson Lakes Trail hike, 111, 113, 130

weather, 10

weeds, noxious, 11

Wells Creek Road, 153, 155

Whatcom Pass–Copper Ridge–Chilliwack River Valley backpacking trip, 75, 77

wheelchair-accessible areas, 68–71, 123–24

White Salmon Road, 152–53

white-water rafting, 85

wildflowers, 9, 72, 125

wildlife, 8–9

Winchester Mountain Lookout–High Pass Trails hike, 52, 54, 75

winter hiking, 156–57, 164–65

Y

Yellow Aster Butte scramble, 84

Yellow Aster Butte–Tomyhoi Lake Trails hike, 49, 51, 75

Z

zero impact camping/hiking, 10–11

About the Author

Mike McQuaide is a freelance writer and photographer who has written several books about hiking and trail-running in the Northwest. He writes frequently for *The Seattle Times* and *Bellingham Herald* and his articles have appeared in magazines such as *Runner's World, Outside, Adventure Sports, Sunset,* and *Trail Runner.* Also an avid triathlete, mountain biker, snowboarder, and mountaineer, McQuaide lives in Bellingham with his wife and young son, Baker, whom they named for the mountain.